Portrait of an Agent

Portrait of a Secret Agent who Knew Kim Philby

Tina Tamman

THOUSAND EYES PUBLISHING

Published by Thousand Eyes Publishing

A CIP catalogue record for this book is available from the British Library.

ISBN 978-0-9930229-0-6

Layout and cover design by Clare Brayshaw

Printed and bound by:

York Publishing Services Ltd
64 Hallfield Road
Layerthorpe
York YO31 7ZQ

www.yps-publishing.co.uk

To my husband Alan

Contents

List of illustrations

27. Cartoon of *The Last of Mrs Cheyney* published in *Postimees*, 19.2.1937
28. Wedding of Anni Oras and Brian Giffey on 1 December 1937
29. Diplomatic corps leaves the presidential palace in Tallinn in 1937 (EFA 2/0-27344)
30. Gen Johan Laidoner (EFA 0-27469)
31. Former British legation at Lai 17, Tallinn, 2014
32. Peter Gallienne hands over credentials to President Päts in June 1940 (EFA 2/0-40733)
33. *Kaitseliit* men and women arrive for an exercise (EFA 5-451)
34. Evald Tart
35. Paul Oras, Anni's cousin
36. Arthur Whittall
37. The Pera Palace, Istanbul
38. Former Estonian legation at 167 Queen's Gate, London, 2006
39. The Shepheard's Hotel, Cairo
40. The Tigris, Baghdad, 1920
41. Al-Rashid Street, Bagdad, 1940
42. Former British legation in Baghdad, 1915
43. Coronation of King Faisal I in Baghdad, 1921
44. Johan Laidoner, 1919 (EFA 10/4-3486)
45. Sandy McKibbin
46. Ants Oras, Anni's brother
47. Brian's drawing to illustrate the slow progress of quadripartite talks
48. The Allied Control Authority building in Berlin
49. The Giffeys in the 1950s
50. Anni Giffey
51. Anni's embroidery class in 1956
52. Anni and Brian eat cake in the 1960s

The photographs are from private collections unless otherwise stated. Every effort has been made to trace the copyright holders of the images used. However, I would welcome any additional information about copyright for further editions of the book.

Introduction

Brian Giffey is not a relative of mine and a few years ago I had not even heard of him. In 2010 I was awarded a PhD for my research into an elusive Estonian diplomat, August Torma, who in 1940 found himself stranded in London after the Soviets had occupied his country. I spent a lot of time trying to establish his circle of friends in order to properly understand his circumstances. Brian's name came up among others. He was expected to attend an Estonian event together with a woman called Anni, so I assumed that they were a couple, but there were no other leads. It was sheer luck and perseverance that led me to their surname and further discoveries. I well remember the excitement when I learnt that Brian had been a British intelligence officer who had spent an unusually long time – eleven years – in Estonia and married an Estonian woman 25 years his junior whose cousin, Paul Oras, had been a Soviet intelligence officer. The two men never met, so Paul makes only a fleeting appearance in this book. However, he certainly contributed to the thrill of my hunt as I was trying to find answers to my questions.

The espionage world is highly secretive, often following its own strange logic. Take the recently published official history of the Secret Intelligence Service (MI6) that begins with a standard disclaimer: "SIS does not disclose the names of agents or of living members of staff and only in exceptional circumstances agrees to waive the anonymity of deceased staff."[1] This leads the reader to expect few names in the hundreds of pages of the book. However, names abound. There are those, for example, of former heads of SIS stations: Harold Gibson, Ronald Meiklejohn and Frank Foley. Even Richard Maasing, an Estonian who was a British agent, gets a mention. Not so, however, Brian Giffey, although he also headed the SIS station in Tallinn, the capital of Estonia. Why has his name been omitted, I wonder?

Puzzlingly, there is an easily recognisable description of him, meant just for the initiated: "an Oxford man who had served with the British Military Mission in south Russia in 1918-19 and had 'considerable experience of producing amateur dramatics'."[2] Why was this sentence included? There are altogether six lines devoted to Brian in this book by Keith Jeffery, while Harry Steptoe, another station head, has been given practically six pages. Brian Giffey died in 1967, he left no children, no young nieces or nephews who might be affected or upset by whatever is said about him – he in fact left no relatives whatsoever. So why not name him? Even his widow died in 2000, eleven years before the publication of Jeffery's book.

Brian Giffey's name, however, is not totally absent from espionage books. Nigel West has mentioned him, consistently calling him "Major Giffey" in his *MI6: British Secret Intelligence Service Operations 1909-45* until, on page 322, he becomes Frank Giffey, which is incorrect.[3] Although Brian had a complicated array of names, Frank was not one of them. Phil Tomaselli has made the logical conclusion in his *Tracing Your Secret Service Ancestors* and called him Chester Giffey.[4] Chester was indeed his first, if not preferred, name. Giffey, without a first name, appears in the autobiography of a fellow spy, Harold "Kim" Philby. The marvellous manipulator's memoir *My Silent War* was first published in New York in the spring of 1968, followed by a British edition a few months later. The latter, however, was an expurgated version. As far as I have been able to establish, the book was translated into Russian only in 1980, and from the expurgated London edition.

Working for SOE in 1941, Philby was given responsibility for staff training. He was downhearted about the trainers available and expressed his disappointment by naming three individuals: "Seasoned secret service officers were in desperately short supply. In practice, they could only have been drawn from SIS. It was clear that if SIS had been approached for suitable instructors, it would have followed time-honoured practice by off-loading duds (if even they could have been spared). It is awesome to think what would have happened to the trainees if they had fallen into the hands of Foley of Berlin, Giffey of Riga, or Steptoe of Shanghai." In the British, expurgated, version the final sentence simply reads as follows: "It is awesome to think what would have happened to the trainees if they had fallen into the hands of such men." The individual names are no longer there, and yet the suggestion of impending calamity has been retained.[5]

Nigel West, Phil Tomaselli and Kim Philby are to my knowledge the only authors who have named the intelligence officer Brian Giffey. West, however, got his first name wrong, Tomaselli, quite understandably, called him Chester and Philby placed him in the wrong capital – Brian was stationed in Tallinn, not Riga (where he spent about a year between 1927 and 1930, learning Russian at the very start of his MI6 career). So why has Brian Giffey fared so badly? Fared badly in the field that prides itself in information gathering. I can't be the only one to believe that only accurate information is worth gathering. To add insult to injury, Philby apparently didn't think much of him, calling him a dud. And the writer

Graham Greene, who at one point also worked for SIS, said that Philby's account of the secret service is devastatingly true. "His character studies are admirable if unkind," Greene concluded.[6] This suggests, even if indirectly, that Philby was right to say that Brian Giffey was a dud.

Philby, however, was a novice in 1941 when he worked together with Brian; he was only 29 against Brian's 54. Why would he pass judgement on a much more experienced officer old enough to be his father? Or perhaps one should ask why Philby needed to name him at all, or any of the three for that matter? This is one of the questions I have been considering when writing this book. Subsequent British editions of Philby's autobiography, as far I have been able to check, have not reinstated the three names.

It is also worth mentioning that the title of Philby's book when it was first published varied slightly. In America things were kept simple: the book had an author – Kim Philby – and a title – *My Silent War*. The British version, however, was published under the title of *My Silent War. The Autobiography of Kim Philby*, as if its authorship was somehow in doubt.

This small variation is a reminder of smoke and mirrors that permeates the world of intelligence. Things are never simple. It has been suggested that Philby's manuscript was heavily censored by the KGB, and yet we know nothing about the British (or American?) editing process. My primary concern is with Brian and my desire to do justice to him, but his work and achievements cannot be properly assessed until the Secret Intelligence Service archives are open to researchers. Is this likely to happen in my lifetime? I doubt it. Jeffery has at least volunteered to explain why a huge amount of SIS archival material has been lost: "In general, the SIS attitude to archives was that they should be kept only if they served some clear operational purpose. Certainly, since no one envisaged that a professional history of any sort would be written, let alone one that might be published, there was no imperative to retain materials for historical reasons."[7] This explanation may not be entirely convincing, but it raises the hope that SIS archivists have learnt their lesson and we can look forward to the day when the archives will indeed be opened because the cellars are full to bursting.

Wesley K. Wark, who analysed the work of Arthur Leslie Nicholson, another colleague of Brian's, was also looking forward to SIS archives opening. Wark was lucky, inasmuch as Nicholson published his memoirs. Also, Kenneth and Peggie Benton wrote about their time in Riga where Nicholson was the head of station. This left Wark with three versions to compare and there was enough overlap to make his comparison meaningful. Having wondered how much work Nicholson actually managed to do, Wark concluded that there was no compelling reason to doubt the veracity of his account. Also, "whatever the precise scale of espionage operations sustained at Riga, the station's performance was clearly rated a success. Nicholson and Kenneth Benton both enjoyed promotions upon their return to London."[8] On the same basis, Brian Giffey must be regarded as a success because he, too, was promoted upon his return to London. He cannot have been a dud, as Philby suggested.

Brian unfortunately published no memoirs although in the 1940s he sat down to make a start. "For years the urge to write has been growing upon me, until it has become a passionate desire. Somebody or something – I forget when – put it in my head that, having seen much of the world and met all kinds of conditions of folk of many races, and having had the good fortune of being in all sorts of queer places at the time of amusing or significant events, I should write of all I have met and all I have seen, and what I made of it. And so I will... This implies that I shall let many a cat out of the bag. See yon enormous sack! It writhes and heaves. God save us all, what mutterings and mewing, what caterwauling and spitting!" Pleased with himself and his opening lines, Brian continued for a while, elaborating on what he had already written until something else took his attention and he put the writing aside. After a break he made another start, then another, leaving all the versions incomplete.

Could Brian have published had he completed? Probably not. It was only in 1977, ten years after his death, that the government allowed former intelligence officers to publish their memoirs. Wartime records had become available under the 30-year rule. Nicholson and Philby were just exceptions that slipped through the net in 1966-68.

The official guidance issued in 1977 reminded potential memoirists to keep in mind the Official Secrets Act and to submit their manuscripts to their former departments for scrutiny.[9] Prof F.H. Hinsley was commissioned to write an official history of wartime intelligence. The news of such openness, however, so horrified Maj Ian G. Menzies whose brother had been the head of SIS up until 1951 that he wrote to *The Times* to say: "On several occasions my brother Sir Stewart Menzies told me that he hoped and expected that nothing would ever be disclosed regarding the operations of his branch."[10] Sir Stewart Menzies also wrote an autobiography before his death in 1968, but it is still kept in the SIS registry as an administrative record and is certainly not for publication.[11]

A number of intelligence memoirs have been published over the years, and some of them make for an excellent read. Leslie Nicholson was a good observer who had a way with words;

the same is true of Kim Philby, Peggie Benton, David Mure and Nigel Clive, to name but a few I've enjoyed. None of them seems to have attracted SIS objection. However, the obituary of Nigel Clive wondered how his book had avoided the fuss that followed the publication of Peter Wright's *Spycatcher* the very same year, 1985. The Crown took Wright's case to court where it claimed that "MI5 and SIS operatives never ventured into print."[12] This suggests that there is still much ambiguity. Can a former intelligence officer publish his reminiscences or not?

Authors of official histories are treading on firmer ground. There are, for example, the four volumes written by Prof Hinsley and, most recently, the impressive tome by Keith Jeffery. The latter's preface says: "The fact that a publicly available history of any sort has been commissioned, let alone one written by an independent professional historian, is an astounding development, bearing in mind the historic British legacy of secrecy and public silence about intelligence matters."[13] However, a glance at Jeffery's endnotes reveals that most of them refer to sources in public, not SIS own, archives. We do not even learn how the SIS archives are organised and what reference system they use.

Even the Foreign Office's relationship with intelligence was mysteriously strained, and might still be. Brian's name, for example, does not appear in any of the annual staff lists the FO used to publish. At the outbreak of war in 1939, however, the FO saw Brian Giffey doing work of "real national importance" in Tallinn. This is claimed in a letter that named him alongside several other passport control officers, all of whom were at that point seen as part of the FO.[14] Brian's name, however, has never appeared on the diplomatic list although this seems to have been the standard practice. When in 1947 the embassy in Baghdad asked London: "Do you generally throughout the world approve the idea that MI6 should be an integral part of the Embassy, and if so, is it the normal practice for all the senior staff to be on the Diplomatic List?", the FO's reassuring answer was "yes".[15] While there is no trace of Brian on this list, he on the other hand appears as an FO employee, Major C.K.O.B. Giffey, in another annual FO publication (index to correspondence) for 1939-40.

Baghdad matters because that was where Brian Giffey was dismissed from the intelligence service in 1944. Wartime Iraq has not attracted much attention in Jeffery's history – the country was sidelined by events – but there were certainly various intelligence organisations in Baghdad treading on each other's toes. Rivalry was rife and so, it seems, was ambiguity. This is exemplified in surviving letters that question the relationship between MI5 and MI6. One diplomat asked another: "Are you entirely happy that these two organisations are not tending to overlap too much?" A colleague replied laconically, "no". The following awkward apology adds piquancy to the letter: "I know it is against our practice to mention names in such a connexion. I have, however, felt compelled to break the rule because it is really almost impossible to explain the situation otherwise. Of course, if you wish in your reply you can just use the initial letter."[16] How were such issues ever clarified, let alone settled? No wonder that another diplomat wondered "whether there has now been any progress in clearing up the question of boundaries between War Office and Foreign Office responsibilities for underground work in Iraq."[17] No reply has come to light.

Brian's relationship with the Foreign Office continued even after his dismissal from MI6. Having been nominally reinstated in the Worcestershire Regiment in 1944 and promoted lieutenant-colonel, Brian represented Britain in the Nazi Arrest and Denazification Sub-Committee in Berlin, part of the Control Commission in Germany, and received his instructions from the Foreign Office. In this job he worked closely together with Frank Foley, who represented MI6. When Brian in 1949 was made redundant because of his age, the letter confirming his redundancy came from the Foreign Office. And it was the Foreign Office that found him that year a liaision job "to the British authorities" at the Association of Ukrainians in Great Britain.

MI6 (or the Foreign Office) even paid him a pension, but evidence is muddled, as are many things to do with intelligence. Or, dare I suggest it, the evidence points to incompetence. It was the Government Communications Bureau that sent Brian a letter about his pension in 1967, two weeks before he died. It said that on reaching the age of 70 on 29 December his pension would increase to £261.13.0 tax free. The amount seems low, but there is a bigger problem with this letter. I hope that Brian, reading it, retained his customary sense of humour and laughed out loud. His birthday was in May, not December, and he had already turned 80. This reality made the amount of £261.13.0 immediately questionable, since the sum had been calculated with "age addition", it said. How did the letter come to be sent at all? When I attempted to locate the Government Communications Bureau, I found that it was yet another cover name for MI6.[18]

There are many unanswered questions. No wonder that the general public wants to read about espionage. Many labour under the illusion that spying is glamorous and exciting, but many simply want to know about the things their governments are not telling them while spending their money. Secrets give rise to suspicion and conspiracy theories, concealment weaves a web of mystery. There are things that the government could easily explain, perhaps starting with some basics. Agents' codenames might make a good start. How were these allocated or did the agents choose their own? How did they avoid duplication? And why did some have several codenames while others had only numbers, no names? Those people died long ago; an explanation is unlikely to hurt. I have also wondered why published books and archives alike render agents' codenames, sometimes also their surnames, in capital letters throughout. This is true of both British and Soviet intelligence records. Can this be a mere coincidence or was there agreement of some sort? Or was it down to Philby whose reports to the Soviets capitalised names? Did he set the template that the Russians have followed ever since?

My book is largely based on Brian's papers and Anni, too, has an important role to play. Her observations filled some of the gaps in Brian's story, her thoughts about Estonia added a human touch to the events that forced the Giffeys to leave the country in 1940. Being much younger than Brian, she became the keeper of the papers after his death. This, however, created another mystery because, for no obvious reason, she destroyed much of the paper that Brian had left. The Giffeys had been keen letter-writers who also kept diaries. During the few brief periods when they were separated they corresponded daily and few of these letters have survived.

Why did Anni destroy so much? It is hard to know, but she may have been overawed by what she understood of her husband's job and the Official Secrets Act. The Foreign Office warned Brian in a letter sent in 1949: "I am also to draw your attention to the provisions of the Official Secrets Act which apply not only during your period of service but also after your appointment has terminated."[19] The letter has survived, so Anni must have read it. What did she make of it? Brian had no secrets from her, even as regard to his intelligence work, and Anni may have been simply confused. It is also not impossible that a friendly face from MI6 turned up at her doorstep to "help" and tell her what she must destroy.

After Brian's death in 1967 Anni was grief-stricken; she was also bound by a promise to prepare his reminiscences for publication. For the next 32 years she hardly went out, spending most of her time in her flat in central London, reading and rereading Brian's letters. She rearranged them into a chronological sequence, retyping what she thought was worthwhile and – hard to believe – destroying the originals in the process. "Today I've been throwing away a lot of old letters and so much of your work. It is difficult to throw away anything you have written, but I must," she wrote, still addressing her dead husband.

"Most of your diaries I must destroy," Anni wrote, "as most are written in Russian or French and I cannot read Russian well enough and anyway the writing in most of them is so small that it is too difficult to try to decypher the writing." This remark is strange because Brian's one and only surviving diary, from 1917, can be read with ease: Brian wrote in a big and clear hand. However, there are some pages of experimentation in the diary. The artistic and polyglot side in him wanted to insert an occasional Greek word, for example. It was not for nothing that Peter Gallienne, the British minister in Tallinn, referred to Brian's "own particular brand of shorthand". Among Brian's scraps that have survived, there are examples of compressed, abbreviated notes, sometimes in a mixture of English and Russian. Was this the style of shorthand that Gallienne mentioned? We will never know. Anni has incidentally referred to a diary that Brian kept in Russian in Iraq of all places. This indicates how much the language meant to him.

"All I've left now are memories, a lot of letters and diaries – and so I kill time by remembering and writing to you," Anni wrote. "I know you'll never read any of it – but I must go on writing to you, as I used to, whenever we were parted – pretend now that you'll come back to me – one day – sometime – somewhere." Anni also started writing her own reminiscences. "I'm no historian, I have no notes, and my Bron [pet name for Brian] is dead – you left me, my darling, almost 22 months ago – quite suddenly, I hope painlessly, we had not even time to say good-bye – and now I'm writing to recall all our happy times, all our life together – I had started writing it when you were in Germany in 1946 – it's now 1969."

Even if Anni was expecting to have a version of Brian's biography published, she went about it the wrong way. She retyped over 300 pages of notes, in places editing them heavily. Not only did she delete many dates and names (or reduced them to initials), but occasionally she omitted chunks of text quite irrationally. Numerous sentences are incomplete. Brian's surviving letters provide a point of comparison as well as evidence of the devastation wrought by Anni. There must have been large quantities of paper to start with. "I can hardly walk in the living room as the floor, table and all chairs are covered with papers and old diaries and books," she wrote in 1968. "The bedroom has got your and my letters on the table and on the floor and lots of clothes here and there, as I had to open trunks – found some clothes which I must give away – only – at the moment must go on sorting the papers."

What is left reminds me of a patchwork full of holes, although I want to believe that Anni's intentions were good and honourable. "I'm still re-writing our old letters – in a shortened form," she wrote at one point. "I think you would have wished me to do it... I know some of the letters are very bitter and unhappy – I'll shorten them, but I must speak the truth and try not to make anyone really unhappy by them – but it's no good to re-write only the happy memories – it would not be the real picture." Whatever she meant by bitter and unhappy letters, none of those has come to light. The paperwork has also travelled extensively and may have suffered losses in the process. Anni died in London. Her niece Tiina Chenon transported the papers to Stockholm where I saw them and had copies made to bring back to London.

Brian was clearly keen on family history; he hoped that it would be published some day. He was good at planning, but he was also his own worst enemy. His plans were unrealistic and he lacked self-discipline. He started well enough (at least on three occasions), chose a title – "Job-in-Hand" – and wrote about twenty pages about his parents and grandparents before straying into many more pages on the history of the American Civil War, a subject that he was passionate about. In doing so he, alas, lost sight of his family. This means that even his family history is incomplete and full of gaps. He has written very little about his school years and has focused on some periods in his soldiering years, leaving others out. There is hardly a reference to his eleven years in Estonia, but there are pages and pages of his love for Anni.

The KGB files in Tallinn have filled some of the gaps by providing information about Brian's agents in Estonia. They also raise the interesting question of provenance. Where did the KGB get all its information from? The answer must be: from Kim Philby. The archive in Tallinn makes it possible to contemplate the other side of the coin, receipt of the information and the uses it was put to. In the light of this wealth of information in Tallinn, there may be a similar KGB hoard in Riga, waiting for future researchers.

Most people know that KGB information cannot be taken on face value, but one can equally wonder whether Brian and Anni can be believed. Did they write truthfully? Their reminiscences seldom overlap, let alone coincide. They usually wrote about different events, and this allows no comparison or corroboration. However, I have been very much encouraged by a few pages that Anni wrote in 1933; they have led me fairly close to believing what Brian and Anni told each other.

When Anni was in Paris before he met Brian, she kept a diary in which she described in repetitive detail how a rising young Estonian sculptor pursued her, bent on the idea of modelling her head. It did not seem credible, not from the way Anni described it: the sculptor was almost laying siege to her hotel. It seemed more like a young girl's exercise in vanity and self-absorption. She, however, had named the sculptor (Ferdi Sannamees) and it was not too difficult to check. Imagine my delight when it turned out that Anni's story was true. Not only did Ferdi Sannamees model her head in Paris, but he even took the trouble

1. Anni Oras's head modelled by Ferdi Sannamees in 1937.

to cast it in bronze on his return to Estonia. He must have thought highly of Anni's looks. The small cast is currently at Tartu Art Museum where I was able to see it. And suddenly Anni seemed much closer to me, more real. I was unexpectedly moved looking at it. The 1930s Estonian art critics liked the work because of the sitter's dreamy expression.[20]

I have aimed to preserve Brian and Anni's original voices by reproducing quotes from their letters and diaries. Notes have been provided if the quotes come from sources in public archives or add an all-important date. Throughout my book I have aimed for clarity and simplicity. The story is complex enough, involves much travel, several countries and a number of individuals. Brian lived in a period during which two world wars were fought, new states emerged and disappeared and borders moved alarmingly. When Brian first went to Iraq, it was called Mesopotamia. Name changes of this kind add complications to an already complicated story. I have generally given preference to modern place names, but have retained Flanders and Mesopotamia. Consistency has at times eluded me because Russia and the Soviet Union, as well as MI6 and SIS, have been used interchangeably. The Soviet security services changed name several times but I have called them the KGB throughout. Even personal names have presented difficulties. Some Russians living in Estonia spelt their names the Estonian way (e.g. Haritonov) and I have retained this form of spelling.

My thanks go to Tiina Chenon in Stockholm for her help with Brian's papers and photographs. Mikael Sylwan did an excellent job of organising the papers for scanning. Another person I want to thank is Wojtek Szatkowski, who was generous with his remarkable detective skills, time and perseverance. Also, Dr Sa'ad Al-Fattal very kindly provided photographs of Iraq from his private collection.

Chapter 1

Beginnings

Brian Giffey believed for most of his life that he was of Welsh and Scottish descent. Admittedly tongue-in-cheek but driven by genuine belief, he wrote in 1944, aged 57: "I am indeed full of good intention to 'tell the truth, the whole truth, and nothing but the truth', s'welp me Gawd. The first two are easy; as for the third, we Welchmen have the unfortunate reputation of being unable to resist telling a good story. It may not be entirely undeserved. I will even admit that our imaginative enthusiasm may enhance the colouring of events. Yet am I Scots on my mother's side with a feeling anent it of responsibility as deep as pride." A similar elusive spirit runs through another of his declarations: "Thank God that I'm half Scots and all my life I've seen clearly what must be done and what I must do. And the Welsh half of me twists and probes and tries again to find a way to do what I know is right that I should try and accomplish." Intriguingly, he found that "the hot Celtic blood will surge up in me from time to time...it's sometimes – on suitable occasions – not a bad thing to let it rip."

His belief about his Celtic origins was misplaced, as he began to realise towards the end of his life. His father was actually German and mother, Canadian. Most of what is known about Brian's background and parentage, however, comes from his reminiscences. These are unreliable by definition, as all personal reminiscences are. I have been able to supplement his information by finding birth, death and wedding certificates, and they support many of the details written down in Brian's big and legible hand. All the same, the evidence is often as deceptive as his belief in his Welshness. Not that Brian was a liar, but he didn't always tell the truth. He was a colourful character who liked high drama.

As a child, Brian was curious about his surname. He asked his father: "What kind of a name is Giffey?" Aged eleven, he was sensitive to teasing at school. His friends at Gymnasium Altona in Hamburg had said that his name "sounded most outlandish to German ears." Brian has described in great detail what followed once he had asked his question. The three Giffeys were eating dessert in the dining room. "My father looked straight at me with the cool and penetrating look that sometimes took the place of the loving warmth or the teasing affection that I was more accustomed to. This look always seemed to me to come from a remote distance. He said, slowly and distinctly: 'Giffey is a Welsh name.' He carefully folded his napkin, rolled it up and pushed it in its ring, rose, turned abruptly and left the room. My mother broke the dead silence by saying: 'Don't ask your father such questions ever again.' I didn't. I was badly taken aback. I felt that I had inadvertently strayed onto ground that was taboo, and I ever after held my peace."

Intimidated and impressed by the incident, Brian was confident about his Welsh origins. His reminiscences often refer to people who are "also Welsh"; he spent his honeymoon in Wales and dreamt of setting up home there. Only much later, in retirement, for reasons not explained, he realised that he had been mistaken all along. In the margins of a draft chapter he scribbled the words: "Founded on a misconception and to be re-written," but never got any further. A quick glance at a modern German dictionary confirms what Brian must have belatedly realised: his conversation with his father had taken place in German and in that language one cannot hear the difference between the words "Waliser" (Welsh) and "Walliser" (from Valais in Switzerland). Brian was not Welsh at all.

Once aware of the misconception, Brian remembered a visit to Switzerland at the age of twelve. "At Lucerne father took us to the monument of the dying Swiss Lion commemorating the massacre of the Swiss Guards of Louis XVI – loyal unto death no less than Leonidas and his 300 Spartans." The memory, previously tucked away at the back of his mind, stirred his sense of history and heroism, but also led him to draw conclusions about his own parentage. "I imagine that his

2. *The Lion of Lucerne (1820) commemorates the bravery of Swiss guards.*

ancestor of that time – as so many men 'du Valais' had been – [was] one of them – probably in the ranks (for I expect the Officers were Frenchmen) – perhaps a Sergeant or Corporal." Brian realised that his father's origins were in Switzerland, not in Wales, and that he came from a line of military men. My own research into the Swiss connection, however, has drawn a blank: I have found no Giffey living in Switzerland today. Also, to confuse the matters further, there is a Swiss German word "Welch" that is used to describe Swiss people of French origin, possibly from the Valais area.

Brian was seventeen when his father died from a heart attack. Otto Giffey senior was only 59. Had he lived longer Brian may have broached the subject of his origins again and learnt more about his background. But in the event, Brian could only remark in his retirement: "I have never met another Giffey. I have heard of four. One, an Innkeeper in Caernarvonshire who, at one time, is said to have kept a pack of Harriers; another, a Sergeant in the London Metropolitan Police. These two were probably Griffiths or possibly Giffin. A third [was] a photographer in Germany. The fourth was a Frenchman."

Brian Giffey was born in London on 3 May 1887, but he was not a Giffey at birth. His birth certificate gives his name as Otto Chester Kurt Brian Petersen, Petersen being his mother Helena's married name. There is no father mentioned, which means that he was born illegitimate at a time when such things mattered. In his teens, while a schoolboy in Germany, he was known as Otto Giffey (as was his father). By the time he graduated from Merton College in Oxford in 1911, he had become Chester Kenneth Otho Brian Giffey. In his reminiscences he has made no reference to his birth name. He has, however, said that his birth weight was 9 lbs 2 oz, the name "Brian" was donated by his English godmother, Constance Haughton, and his maternal grandfather, Chester Aldrage (Aldridge) Gorton, "had chosen Chester as his contribution to my extraordinary collection of Christian names." He also said that he had a French godmother, Anne de Rochefoucauld de la Hauardrie.

Otto Giffey senior (full name Georg Werner Otto Giffey), Brian's father, set up in business in Hamburg in 1883 when he was 39. "I had it from my mother that, born a landowner in the Altmark and after an eventful and improvident youth, my father had taken to business comparatively late in life," Brian recalled. A schoolfellow of Brian's remembered Otto Giffey as a man who was known to be ill but not complaining. "I remember him as a drinker, with a huge, hooked, red-veined nose, who was always looking for an opportunity for his loud and hearty laugh. He liked to dine well, and now his son's friend, too, was quickly invited to join in. The building adviser Goebel from Altona often came, Senator Harbeck, and some men from the Hamburg stock exchange. Good wine was drunk and jokes, both gross and lighthearted, were told," the friend, Hans Blunck, recalled.[1] He described Giffey senior as neat, precise and imposing. Brian loved his father. "While he lived I was the apple of his eye," he said.

Hamburg, with its Hanseatic League trading background, was doing well at the end of the 19th century. A free port (*Speicherstadt*) was established, old houses in the area were pulled down and new warehouses were built. Otto Giffey senior, a shrewd man, took advantage of the booming shipping trade. There was money to be made from insuring ships' cargo coming from distant lands. He set up an insurance company at Brandstwiete 3/1, a stone's throw from the free port. The building has not survived, but the company surprisingly has. It still operates under its founder's name, if from a different address, and belongs to a completely different group of people.

3. Speicherstadt in Hamburg, 2013.

The founder's magnificent portrait is displayed on the company website; it also hangs in the office where he is thought to have been English. Otto Giffey was a remarkable man, as confirmed by Brian in his reminiscences: "No one could meet my father and fail to feel that before him stood a Chieftain. More I fancy: the descendant of many generations of free men of the mountains; men primitive perhaps in their earlier ideas and habits, but with a tradition of command and of responsibility in every vein."

Clinging to his belief in his ancestry, Brian got muddled. Generations of free men of the mountains is a reference to Wales, but who was it who came to Germany from Wales? He has said of his father that "with neither experience, money nor influence behind him, in a business of which he knew nothing and in a country – the Hansestadt Hamburg – in which he arrived a stranger, he worked up from nothing to affluence as Head of a Marine Insurance Agency which he had started as a one-man show." But if this applies to Otto Giffey, why did Brian choose the words "country" and "stranger", as if his father had arrived directly from Wales? Otto Giffey was in fact born in Salzwedel, about 70 miles southeast of Hamburg, no great distance at all. And Otto's father, Johann Christoph Giffey, had been a landowner in the Altmark, which is in the area, so how did Wales fit in?

Busily weaving a myth about his origins, Brian elsewhere ascribed the journey to Germany to Otto Giffey's father, who "had left the coast of Wales, and ships and the sea, behind him and gone far inland in a strange country. It seems a freak of fortune that mine, who until then knew nothing of the sea and ships, should have made his living by them. With me both have been a passion all my life; and if, as I hope, I shall end my days, when the time comes, in the Land of my Fathers the wheel will have come full circle." (Brian was actually cremated in London.)

Brian's interest in ships goes back to his father and childhood in Hamburg. Years later he remembered "the quays where we used to board little ships – passengers and general cargo – to go to England. 'Navvies' (General Steam Navigation Company) to Harwich or St Catherine's dock (London); GER [Great Eastern Railway] Coy's 'Staveley' and others to Grimsby." Brian went on to lovingly record the measurements and technical details of a paddle steamer he was travelling on in Mesopotamia; he owned a yacht, Kittiwake II, in Estonia and wrote lengthy descriptions of his days out sailing in Berlin.

Teenage years, and pocket money, encouraged Brian's curiosity and enterprising spirit. Hans Blunck, who attended the same imposing Gymnasium Altona as Brian did, was attracted by his friend's unusual interests. Brian knew things he had not even heard of; he had the knack of finding books that were out of the ordinary. One of the books demonstrated "the miracles the human body was capable of when rigid or under command. There was also a discourse about spiritualism, another about thought transference, which seemed quite meaningful to us, wanting to try this out on our class teacher. I learnt to breathe like a yogi and tried to take control of my schoolmates with my captivating glance. Fortunately we gave up this nonsense after a while, when we had become bored by it, or Giffey's mother hid the books."[2] Having saved up his pocket money, Brian ordered from America a four-volume work on hypnosis and suggestion. This changed Hans's perceptions: "Previously I had believed everything said about this to be mad lies, but now I buried myself in it. For one day, so the compiler assured us, I would with this training, that is, staring at a crystal ball and deep breathing, be able to oblige everybody around me to do my will."[3]

When Brian was given a printing press for Christmas, Hans saw it as "the most exciting thing" because he had been secretly composing poems. "So we two decided that we would publish a newspaper – wouldn't I be able to get one of my own poems published? I was burning for the moment. But my friend wanted me only as an assistant printer, he would determine the content of the newspaper from his own works. He began a novel, and I had to set the type. He slipped in a poem – ah, I was too late to admit my secret wish; Otto had used up all the space. He kept consoling me 'in the next edition', and I contented myself, avid and full of expectation. So I began printing but pressed too hard, and ruined the whole newspaper! But I was irreplaceable, and in his enthusiasm my friend forgave me everything."[4] It is a curious irony of fate that

Hans Blunck became a writer who went on to publish several books, including memoirs; his name appears in German reference books, while Brian Giffey never published as much as a single book.

Hans was much impressed by the Giffey household at Eggersallee 6 in Altona, a leafy suburb of Hamburg. "I have a lot to thank the Giffeys' house for," he said, "it's good when one is young to see flexibility and free hospitality, and to learn to turn and to answer. The first contact with the other life, the one that in riper years one should live and master, taught me to behave naturally among other people, as well as to differentiate between useful words and people and the cautious world of rank... I was most attracted at the Giffeys

4. The Giffey house at Eggersallee 6, Altona, Hamburg, 2013.

by the library, which contained completely different things from my mother's bookcase of English classics... (including descriptions of India, life in Canada and China). There was a whole new world to be won!... I learnt in the Giffey house, as the son's always welcome companion, to maintain conversation and to participate in company..."[5]

Brian was known as Otto Giffey, not Brian, and the boys spoke German to each other. There was, however, something unusual, even foreign, about Brian that attracted Hans. His ear tuned to languages and keen to improve his own English, Hans observed cultural tension in the Giffey household. He was aware that Brian's mother spoke only English with her son while the father "wanted to make a German of him". Brian's mother "saw him as the son of an Englishwoman" and there was no doubt in her mind as to her son's nationality, Hans noted. Herself "an Englishwoman born in Canada, she made no secret of the fact that she considered Germany a place of only temporary residence." Hans described the mother as an eccentric woman, invariably dressed in riding clothes because of her love of horses. All the same, she seemed a good mother, he concluded.[6] In the light of his language observations it is not surprising that soon after Brian's father died in 1904, his business was sold and Helena Giffey and her son moved back to England. The decision might have saddened Otto Giffey, but would not have surprised him. He was very much aware that his son Otto was called Brian in English and even inscribed a photograph accordingly. Brian on the other hand has mentioned a longing to return to Britain "where to win my place had been my burning ambition." He obviously decided early on to be English, not German.

5. Otto Giffey's grave at Ohlsdorf cemetery, Hamburg, 2013.

6. Otto Giffey's gravestone, 2013.

Brian's mother was born in Quebec as Helena (Alena) Ella Adelaide Nancy Gorton on 10 July 1844. Nominally her parents were Chester Gorton and Adaline (or Adeline) Wells who, however, had no children of their own. Helena was the result of a union between Chester and a (nameless) actress of Scottish-Irish descent "with a one-eighth strain of Red Indian blood". The fact that Adaline accepted the baby born out of wedlock as her own was in Brian's view "surely a broadminded act in the eighteen-forties." "My grandfather," Brian said, "like most of us, Gordons and Giffeys alike, could never resist the allure of a well-turned ankle and what went above it – a pair of fine eyes, a pair of fresh and well-formed lips, a wayward curl blowing in the breeze, and so forth." Chester's relationship with his wife was strained. "The affair of my mother's birth and adoption seems to have steadied him for years, at least outwardly – but it could not last," Brian concluded.

Chester moved to London in 1863, leaving his wife behind, but taking his daughter along. Helena was 26 at the time. Chester, who had been an engraver in the USA, set himself up as a chemist and perfumer at 397 City Road, Islington. This actually meant selling shampoo, hair colour and dandruff remover ("Safe to Use, Certain to Act"). A man of grand plans, like Brian, he became a naturalised British subject in 1868 because he intended to stay in Britain and acquire property.[7]

While Chester's business prospered, Helena was causing concern. As a child she had been a "red-haired daredevil" and tomboy, and now she failed to settle down. She had already entered into a short-lived relationship with a Presbyterian minister in the United States. In England she first married a man by the name of Weir. He was a good horseman and was comfortably off, but, according to Brian, he "did not possess the tact and skill to tame one of Diana's huntresses of my mother's kittle quality." The marriage was dissolved. A few years later, in 1881, Henry Frederick William Petersen, a university lecturer, arrived on the scene. He became Helena's third husband. Chester witnessed the wedding in Wirral. However, like her previous marriages, this one did not work out either.

Brian has not said when and how Helena met Otto Giffey senior. Sent by her father to Hanover to "finish" her education, Helena may have travelled via Hamburg and met her future husband there. She certainly spent enough time in Germany to speak the language fluently, if ungrammatically, as Brian pointed out. Meanwhile there is no evidence that Otto Giffey had any reason to visit London, but he certainly knew English (and even Greek) as a photograph caption testifies. Brian's parents were both aged 43 when their union produced a baby, their only child. Otto Giffey was a batchelor, Helena, however, was still married to Petersen, so the couple had no option but to wait. Brian was ten years old by the time his parents were able to tie the

7. Baby Brian with father.
Otto Giffey senior wrote the dedication in English (and knew that in that language his son was called Brian) but inserted a Greek word, meaning "child". Brian, too, was known to use occasional Greek words in his English sentences.

knot in London on 28 August 1897. And who is there to say that Helena did (or did not) obtain a divorce from Petersen?

"Some three months after I was born my mother left London to rejoin my father and bring his son to him," Brian said. This involved a sea crossing. "This was our second sea voyage within six months. So much travel by sea before my birth and in early infancy may have further encouraged an inherited and constitutional love for the sea and ships. We sailed in one of the old 'Navvies' – ships of the General Steam Navigation Company, small coasters that carried a dozen or so passengers and 700 to 1500 tons of general cargo between the London river and all the ports of Western Europe," Brian wrote in his reminiscences.

Another voyage was undertaken by Helena, who went to the States trying to trace Petersen for a divorce. "She had been away for a year and found that father wanted her to share him with a young woman with whom he had fallen in love during mother's absence. It cost my father most of my mother's love, me very much of it, and the poor girl her life. I only met her once. She was a Professor's daughter in the upper twenties. I do not think that I ever knew her name. My father was never one to beat about the bush, and explained the whole situation to mother when we met at Ostende... My mother utterly refused to accept the situation as proposed by father. She turned into a fury rather than the fond mistress and loving mother she had been. For some years life was not too easy."

Brian's first 19 years were spent in Hamburg, with occasional short spells in England. The 1891 British census records confuse by listing a Nancy Gorton at 397 City Road in London. Nancy was one of Brian's mother's middle names, the woman's age corresponds to that of Helena, but her birthplace is given as London and she is described as Chester's wife. No information about Chester's remarriage has come to light, although he is known to have employed a housekeeper who was also his mistress. Too much of a coincidence perhaps to find a mistress of his daughter's age who was called Nancy Gorton. Could it have been Helena? According to what she told her son, Chester quite doted on her after her baby's birth, "surrounded her with every comfort and brought her every delicacy and pleasing trifle he could think of and afford". However, there is no suggestion that their relationship was anything other than loving affection between father and daughter. But if the woman was indeed Helena, where was the 4-year-old Brian? His name does not appear on the census form.

Who knows what kind of checks were possible in those days? Chester Gorton felt it necessary to seek naturalisation in Britain, declared his circumstances and personal details, but his age in documents varies. He said his date of birth was 18.3.1822, but when he died on 22 February 1902, his age was given as 77, not 79, as it should have been. A couple of years is perhaps insignificant, not worth worrying about, but there is a bigger shift in Helena's dates. She was born on 10 July 1844, but when she married Petersen, her age was given as 30, which moves her birth to 1851. Perhaps she simply wanted to seem younger, since Petersen was only 27? By the time she married Giffey she was two years older, as if born in 1849. However, when she died on 27 December 1936, her age was correctly given as 92, in keeping with the original 1844 birth.

Brian remembered how grandfather Chester came to see them off when he and Helena left for Hamburg. He "tipped me nobly," Brian said, suggesting that he was old enough to know the value of money. "He was always most generous, sending me magnificent presents; a model yacht that lasted many years and won races, and a glorious steam-driven Great Eastern model railway engine, both from Bassett and Lowkes, High Holborn, [they] are unforgettable." Brian also said that his grandfather "had great charm of manner, an understanding as deep as his love of his fellow-man, and was generous to a fault."

When grandfather Chester died, however, Brian related the circumstances only from his mother's point of view. Helena had not written to her father from Hamburg for some time and when she did, her letters were returned. This is how she discovered that "her gentle, loving father had died. She never knew when or of what cause, or even where he lies buried." Brian also referred to the mysterious housekeeper-cum-lover. "His passionate friend, the latinist Minister's daughter, had disappeared none knew whither. If she had taken his inheritance with her, that – apart from certain of his pictures and his favourite books – worried my mother little compared with the knowledge that his fortunes had, before the end, declined – and the suspicion that, at his death, he may have been left to the care of strangers, lonely and in want." The sentiment sounds false, particularly since Chester's bankruptcy was declared in 1891, with details published in *The London Gazette*, and he died in 1902. It is unlikely that Helena knew nothing about her father's financial difficulties.[8] She had visited London at least once, in 1897, when her marriage to Giffey was solemnised. Chester's fortunes must have been going downhill for years.

Brian was fifteen when his grandfather died, but he has not said a word about his own feelings, much as he generally held him in high esteem. Even if he thought that the ageing Chester was no longer a successful businessman, he has not said so. He has also overlooked another discrepancy, seemingly oblivious to it altogether: Chester's surname was Gorton, not Gordon, as Brian consistently wrote.

Chester Gorton was in fact a distant descendent of Samuel Gorton, the religious dissenter who gained some fame as an early English settler in the United States and colonist of Rhode Island. The Gorton family produced an impressive fat tome on the lineage, listing also Chester Gorton, his wife and daughter. Helena, however, must have had her own reasons for opting for Gordon at some point. The 1850 US census lists Chester, 26, an engraver, Adaline, 28, and Helena, 4, as the Gortons in the town of Le Roy, County of Genesee, New York State. Ten years later the census shows Chester as a mere "day laborer" in Rock Island, Illinois. The family had moved home, probably because of the court-enforced sale of Chester's property. The 1860 US census taker incidentally turned all three into Gordons. Once in England, Helena may have found Gordon more manageable. After Brian's birth in 1887 all her documents show her maiden name as Gordon. Meanwhile Chester remained Gorton all his life.

Brian would have rejoiced had he realised that Samuel Gorton was a distant relative. He was always on the lookout for heroes and models, frequently quoting the Classics. When, in 1945, he first felt the urge to write his reminiscences, he enthusiastically listed the heroes whose histories he would like to write: "King David, Xenophon and Kallikrates, Hannibal, C. Julius Caesar and Germanicus, Caratacus, Llewellyn the Great and Owen Glyn Dwr, Wallace, Henri of Navarre, Robert E. Lee and many others." Samuel Gorton was not perhaps in the same league, but Brian was genuinely proud of his ancestry and lovingly retold the story of his mother's great-grandfather, Tom Gordon, the spelling he believed to be correct. Tom Gordon married the daughter of a Hector McDonald in Aberdeenshire; the young couple then left Scotland for Quebec. This was proof enough for Brian to conclude that Helena was Scottish. Even

Brian's army form says that his mother was Scottish and his father Welsh.

Brian was very close to his mother whom he has described as small, slim, elegant and strong-willed. She was a skilled horsewoman and a marvellous cook. "She had a wonderfully fresh and clear mind and many live interests and sympathies: a love and true and vivid appreciation of books, deep love of beauty in all its forms and of nature, particularly of landscape and perhaps most of all of woods and trees, a profound interest in people and a great love of animals, especially dogs and horses... She had a sharp wit and was a great conversationalist." The stories Helena told her son about her own childhood, involving horses, dogs, a parrot and oysters, were memorable – clear evidence of her skill as a storyteller. Brian lapped them up, remembered them for years to come, possibly even honed his own storytelling skills on those of his mother.

Meanwhile he was very much aware of the flaws in his mother's character. "She was warmhearted and impulsive, but most easygoing and careless," Brian recollected. His father had once told her: "You have that sort of tact, Helena, that enables you to say the things that hurt most." Without a trace of rancour Brian has referred to a childhood incident that involved "the whalebone riding switch which was her favourite instrument of correction." And yet he remained full of admiration for her. "My mother, like all her kin, developed slowly; she was almost 43 when I was born; she rode a horse for the last time when she was 84; her hair did not start greying noticeably until she was about 80; and she lived to be 92 and more." He was grateful for her guidance. "My mother certainly introduced me to a very large proportion of the books that have given me the greatest pleasure and have most influenced my life; her taste remained amazingly catholic to the end of her days."

About his mother's marriages Brian has been most chivalrous. "She always told me that she liked men well enough when she was young, and if one was nice-looking and a good friend and comrade, she felt that companionship for life might be a splendid affair. But that – until my governor came along – she could never abide it if they came too close. All this might sound like moonshine to some, and like cheating to others; but I can well believe that my mother remained essentially virginal for years, and that her first three husbands were neither the men to sweep her off her feet, nor had the tact and fire to make love to her and win her." Otto Giffey, Brian's "governor", was at last the man to win Helena's heart. He may have also provided her with much-needed stability. When he died,

the widow and son were financially secure because, as Brian put it, "My father left us – my mother and me – well off."

Having returned to England, Helena chose to set up home at the village of Stetchworth close to Newmarket. She bought an old house, The Firs (or the Orme Firs) that "stood among cedars, firs and other trees on the very last ridge of the Chilterns". It has survived and is now called the Mill House. When Brian first visited in December 1908, he listened

8. *Young Brian with father in their garden at Eggersallee around 1898.*

with pleasure to the winds singing high in the tall trees. He was less happy with the location but knew that Helena loved horses and was a passionate gambler. "The Firs, and Stetchworth, were in East Anglia, and on the wrong side of Britain, and the neighbourhood of Newmarket, the central mart of racing and – alas – the Mater's Mecca, were not of my choosing. The place was far from the sea and not even near the river," he noted ruefully. Stetchworth itself he liked. Unexpectedly it provided confirmation of his Welsh origins. When he first arrived a neighbour quipped: "Giffey, that's a Welsh name, isn't it?"

Brian's first years in England were spent in Oxford, but at Stetchworth he "came to feel that the old house had a personal individuality, that became my friend, too and I feel so still. The Firs, Stetchworth, were the first home I had known. I desired with all my heart to make it permanent and did not see why it should not be – though I always feared its loss. There I longed to take a worthy place among my fellows and hoped to make it a family seat." Ten years later, however, the house was gone, gambled away. "The sporting old mater went security for Estelle and that horrible push to the tune of £800, and the Orme Firs had to be mortgaged," Brian said laconically. How much of a financial burden the loss was for him personally is hard to judge, but even in 1936 when he took early retirement he may have thought of his mother: he wanted to claim a half-pension to clear "family debts". That was the year Helena died, in a London care home.

Brian knew early on that he wanted to be an army officer. His father encouraged him, as an early dressing-up photograph shows. When Brian joined Merton College in 1907, he chose to go for the pass degree as a "university candidate for the Regular Army" and not to seek honours. He had a good start because the examinations he had taken at Gymnasium Altona in Greek, Latin, maths and German satisfied the college and he was exempted from entrance exams. At Merton he studied a range of subjects, including English law, French language and literature, and "Elements of Military Engineering and Military Topography".

9. Gymnasium Altona, Hohenzollernring 57, Hamburg, 2013.

Gymnasium Altona had at one point been a "Latin School" and was still officially called Christianeum Altona when Brian attended. The respect for the Classics it developed in Brian was further encouraged at Merton. His surviving letters and notes testify to a grand and heroic writing style. A British diplomat, J.D. Gregory, has explained the influence of Latin and Greek studies on his own writing. It is likely that Brian may have experienced something similar. "When I was at school," Gregory said, "it was the custom, as I suppose it was in most schools, to set subjects for Latin Verse about which the average schoolboy was almost wholly incapable of writing one word of sense. I know that I was. For instance, we were constantly asked to write elegiacs on such themes as 'The Romance of Tragedy' or 'Unrequited Love' or some similar abstraction which meant nothing to us whatsoever. However, we were undefeated, as befitted boys of our spirit, and we had a method of attack, which was never known to fail. With a *Gradus ad Parnassum* in one hand and a gnawed pen in the other, we began, after the preliminary 'Oh, Muse, come to my aid'".[9]

Graduation from Merton came in November 1911 and Brian was awarded a BA. A significant name change occurred at Oxford. Having enrolled in 1907 as Otto Chester Kurt Brian Giffey, he claimed in March 1911 that his name had been entered incorrectly and his given names should be Chester Kurt Otto Brian. The records were amended accordingly. By the time he graduated, however, he had become Chester Kenneth Otto Brian Giffey, the name that he proudly bore to the end of his life.[10] Most of his life he was known as (Major) C.K.O.B. Giffey. The shedding of "Kurt" at Oxford must have severed his links with Germany. Kenneth probably referred to Doris and Kenneth (no surname) with whom Helena and young Brian spent a long summer holiday at Scarborough. Otto (or Otho), however, lingered. It probably reminded Brian of his father – and it wasn't strictly German.

Only once in his reminiscences has Brian referred to the legal difficulties involving his name changes. He began with the obstacles his parents had in their intention to marry, then went on to describe his own dealings with "old Negus" in Oxford. To get the full benefit of his words one needs to know that Brian was rather attached to No 2 Vernon Place, Bloomsbury, London, where his mother had been staying around the time of his birth. It belonged to a Mrs Mayhew who was known in some circles as a spiritualist. Thought transference was also of interest. These were the fields that had coincidentally fascinated Brian in his teenage years in Hamburg. The reminiscences below, however, refer to the time when he was ten years old and in London. This makes the year 1897 – the year his parents finally got married. It also needs to be said that No 2 Vernon Place was close to Gray's Inn where the cleverest lawyers were to be found.

"In old Negus' office, only about 100 yards North of where Mrs Mayhew's house still stood, I typed 'I have an apple' under the guidance of one of the old chap's clerks, on the first typewriter I had ever set eyes upon, when I was ten years old, the while my parents were wheedling and bribing the benign old sinner into helping them to get married at last, though the Dear only knew whether the Mater's last previous husband was alive or dead. Or did they pull it off by nothing but cajolery and charm? After all, the paternal old rascal only accepted a simple lunch in my digs in Teddy Street at Oxford, bare travelling expenses and a fee of two guineas for the amazing feat of persuading the War Office to accept me as a candidate for the Regular Army under my father's name, when my birth certificate had given me

10. Brian Giffey as a teenager.

that of my mother's third husband and a rather different set of Christian names." Writing this years later when No 2 Vernon Place was no longer standing, Brian referred to it as "the all-important appointment with old Negus that was to open the road to a Commission in my Regiment to me."

This all-important, if obscure, sequence of events led Brian to record in 1964, when he was 77 years old: "The great and only achievement of my life has been that, though the son of a father of French-Swiss descent (*du canton de Valais*), but of German nationality, I managed to be accepted for a commission in the British Army at a time when things were already hotting up for World War I."

One regret that Brian returned to again and again was his lack of any proper family. When in 1946 his wife Anni was missing the "tender comfort and unquestioning support" of her mother, Brian told her: "You see, my mother wasn't like that. My father died when I was 17. Uncle Alfred and Aunt Jessie were not my own relations, indeed, I never had any. I've had good friends who have helped me – from time to time, in my greatest need: first and foremost Frank Stacke and Bowring whose friendship was entirely disinterested, pure giving without return." He also named Col Dunlop and Peter Gallienne in a similar spirit. "But none of them belonged to me, and *mo creagh*! How I have longed for succour, for help and strength, outside me, the strong support, advice, the loving protection of one's own folk and family – the loving understanding of father, of mother – the unquestioning comradeship and loyalty of one's own clan."

Chapter 2

Wounded in Flanders

Having completed his degree course at Merton in 1911, Brian Giffey became a regular army officer (2nd lieutenant). He joined the Worcestershire Regiment, and this gave him what he wanted – a sense of belonging. "The Regiment is a unit, intensely clan, family conscious, wherever it goes," he said, proud to have been accepted. "I, without a Public School or even an English Education behind me, very poor at games in consequence, without County roots or background anywhere and finally coming in

*11. 2nd Lieutenant
C.K.O.B. Giffey.*
Courtesy of Mercian Regiment
Museum (Worcestershire).

at the age of 24 could hardly have hoped to last out at any more conventional Corps until the beginning of the War. Finally I had no influence whatever and knew nobody." The regiment he had chosen was very much to his liking – unpretentious but one of the best. The standards were high but "unusually tolerant". Only the pay was poor at £120-150 per annum.

The years leading up to the First World War were spent in Egypt which Brian absolutely loved. The regimental history views this period as "two pleasant years" during which the "most notable events of military importance included minor riots at Alexandria, the organisation and training of successive Camel Corps troops at the Central School in Cairo, and the manouvres of the little British Army of Occupation in heat and dust across the desert near the Pyramids. Besides those events, the tour in Egypt was notable for much hospitality at Alexandria to the visiting warships of many nations."[1]

Brian's reminiscences recall the musical pleasures of Cairo. "Peter Ruck and I went to see 'Madame Butterfly' at the magnificent Opera House on the Place Mehemet Ali. We were both terrifically impressed by a gorgeous show. I have always tremendously admired Puccini, but remember telling Peter that I would never see Mme Butterfly again – it was too grievously harrowing – never, never, never," he repeated for effect. "Some of Peter's and my happiest hours were spent at a large open-air music-hall on the same bank of the Nile. There was one particularly delightful turn by two Frenchmen as a Sergeant and a Trumpeter, 'Sonnez la Soupe'." Already a homemaker, Brian bought wall hangings and lamps to make his quarters more comfortable. At one stage he even hired a piano.

Brian's 1st battalion was brought back to England in October 1914, by which time the war had started. In a surprise move Brian married a German girl at Stetchworth, his mother's home, merely four days after docking at Liverpool. There may not have been the time for the banns, nor was there apparently an opportunity for Brian to reflect on the consequences of his actions. Claire Maria Eleanor Scholz-Leclere, his bride from Hamburg, was a family friend, possibly even a distant relative.

Brian had known her for a number of years. At the time of the 1911 British census Claire had stayed at Stetchworth and Helena, Brian's mother, who filled in the census form, duly declared her visitor. Now, on 20 October 1914, Helena attended her son's wedding ceremony but she, too, may not have fully realised the implications.

It took a local busybody by the name of Sherman to ask questions before the penny dropped. Sherman, an upright citizen, wanted to know whether Brian had obtained his commanding officer's permission to marry a German, and Brian had to admit that he had not. Much later, looking back, Brian concluded that he had been simply immature. "I was a pretty poor specimen of a young man, soft, self-centred and selfish, self-indulgent to a degree, a snob and an ass... I learnt little at Oxford... The Regiment taught me more."

Brian was grounded in Cornwall for over a month while his regiment was sent to France. "Sherman said that, as my mother had had extensive German interests and connections and I had just married a German lady, he would feel that it was his duty to report the circumstances to the War Office unless I reported all the facts to my CO on the following day," Brian said. He had no alternative but to talk to the commanding officer, Lascelles, who passed the news further up the chain. Lascelles was not kind – a friend found his behaviour unspeakable. As a result, "while no doubt further enquiries were being made it was decided to leave me at home with the 5th Reserve Bn. at Millbrook (on the R. Tamar) in Cornwall – until the authorities had satisfied themselves that Claire, and I, could be trusted."

Claire, two years older than Brian, remained a special person in Brian's life while she lived, and even beyond; she was as special as his regiment. Brian's allegiance to the regiment, however, might be easier to understand than Claire.

Brian's admiration for the Worcestershire has been very specific. His fellow officers had attended public school and this in his opinion set them apart. Public school was something marvellous that he had been deprived of. Sportsmanship, fairness, tolerance, self-control and ability to judge and meet situations were things that his fellow officers had mastered as a matter of course, while he had to learn it all in adulthood. Theirs were the skills he was lacking. He looked up to several officers and mentioned in particular Lt Veasey who was a born leader and Capt E.B. Conybeare, a true hero. Both inspired him, and both fell in Flanders. "One has got used to one's dearest pals getting killed," Brian wrote.

Claire, by contrast, remains shadowy and refuses to come to life. Brian has spent many words on her, but they describe his own thoughts, mostly anguish and soul-searching, not her. The couple spent relatively little time together, but Claire was often on Brian's mind. And yet, she never acquired a visual form or specific features apart from dark hair and two pigtails. Brian has referred to no incidents that might reveal aspects of her character. She was always there, around him, but formless, non-specific. Her presence moved into the foreground whenever Brian was ill with fever. Fever heightened Brian's concerns, made him agonise, while leaving it unclear whether he was worried for Claire or for himself.

The bond between Brian and Claire was extraordinarily strong, even after they drifted apart and when, years later, they divorced. There is no doubt that Brian loved her, at least at the beginning, but their relationship was different from the boy-meets-girl pattern; it was more like kinship.

What made him marry her when he did? The likeliest explanation is Brian's desire to protect her, but his fellow officers responded to the marriage with a greater display of public-spiritedness than this explanation would warrant. Brian's best friend, Captain FitzMaurice Stacke, told him: "All the (Officers of the) Regiment say that your marriage, Brian, reflects the greatest credit on you." Brian's response to Stacke's comment fails to clarify the matter: "I really do not know how by doing the only thing I could do in bare decency I deserved credit, but chaps already in the Regiment certainly treated me as if they liked me better." The regiment must have known more about Claire's circumstances than Brian's notes reveal. "Liked me better" and "bare decency" might even suggest that Claire was pregnant, but their baby was stillborn a whole year later.

When, in the 1930s, Brian at last found the love of his life, Anni, and married her, he insisted that she should befriend Claire. In 1945, when he was posted to Germany and Anni stayed behind in England, he insisted, quite implausibly, that the two women should share a house. When tensions arose, Brian tried to pacify Anni from afar by writing several pages about Claire before they got married. "She did love me, with all of her devotedly, I was her God; I was always not faithful to her, she followed me blindly, left everything without any hope of marriage. And when the war changed everything and we did get married, after less than two years of terrible anxiety and perfect happiness combined, when she was expecting our baby, I let her down. God forgive me! Left her to play with someone else. Can you imagine how you would have felt about it in a land nothing as friendly as is about you now, far from your own folk?"

He had chosen his words carefully, trying to make Anni think of herself being far from her homeland. And Claire in 1914-18 was not only a foreigner in England but a German, and there was a war on. Was there perhaps a danger that Claire might be interned unless Brian married her? On the other hand, what made him write that Claire followed him blindly, without any hope of marriage?

12. Capt Edward Langley Bowring.

Courtesy of Mercian Regiment Museum (Worcestershire).

Capt Edward Langley Bowring stood up for Brian when he was at last allowed to join his regiment after the wedding. He was the man Brian owed to more than to any other man; he was "a natural champion of the underdog", as Brian put it. It was at Bailleul in Flanders in mid-December 1914 that a rumour was circulating about "a 2nd Lieut who was a German spy" about to join them. Bowring, however, believed that Brian should be given a chance to prove himself and asked him to be included in his C company.

"And that is how Bowring, God bless him, gave me the first instance of his unfailing generosity, which brought me his wonderful friendship," Brian said warmly.

Brian was to remember Bowring's friendship for years to come. He and Anni visited him in Feltham in the early 1940s and found him ageing rapidly. When in 1946 Brian had leave he wanted to spend some time with Bowring and his wife. "You have no idea what Bowring did for me," he reminded Anni. "He stood up for me and saw that I got fair play before he ever set eyes on me. He taught me most I learnt about soldiering in Europe in wartime, and immeasurably much about life, and essential decency, besides – much more than he would realise.

He supported me and gave me strength throughout. And when he left he – in face of strong opposition – saw to it that I got his company."

After their visit in December 1946 Brian wrote to Bowring to thank him for his hospitality and past support. He added that the ten months in Flanders in 1914-15 had been "the most intensely vital and most closely remembered time of my life. For more than half of it I was your Subaltern; for the remainder I had the honour of commanding your company. I owed that command to you, and if I didn't make an absolute hash of it I owed that too to your teaching – very largely by example – to the C company tradition you had built up."

New to war, Brian experienced the full horrors of Flanders. The infamous waterlogged trenches, the constant fire and unburied corpses are well-known. The regimental history has added some practical touches by explaining the rota system. "In the front trenches there was little possibility of rest or sleep, and it was soon realised that three days and nights of constant wakefulness and strain were about the useful limit of human efficiency. Consequently it became customary for battalions to be relieved every three days or thereabouts. During the first winter battalions were paired for that purpose and relieved each other every three days in the same line of trenches."[2]

A fellow officer, Lt Edward Barton, has fondly remembered being billeted in Bethune during their days off. Life in the town was more or less normal, he said, with schools, shops and cafes open as a matter of course. "One pleasure was a visit to the barber's shop to have a haircut and shampoo followed by a friction. This was the first time I had had one of these, generally they were given with some reddish liquid, but there was also an Eau de Cologne friction, this was like a freezing electric shock which shrank your scalp so much that you could hardly shut your eyes, it was all a luxurious pleasure."[3]

In the trenches steel helmets were worn and Barton did not like those. "They were horrible things to wear and made you slightly less efficient. I grudgingly admit though that I was thankful I had one on when a shrapnel bullet pinged against my helmet," he said. There was also the constant battle of keeping "trench feet" at bay. "While in trenches you remained booted and dressed, perhaps an occasional foot inspection took place, of one or two men at a time." A typical day started with breakfast. "Every officer had a soldier servant, at that time there was no false feeling of shame in that name, and it caused no resentment; after all, we were all in service, both officers and men were servants of the Crown." It was the servant who had to ensure that cooking was done without smoke, or else it would be "bacon and bullets", as Barton put it. He recalled that "there would be a beautiful smell of frying bacon for some time." Tea, sugar, Ideal Milk and jam were available. "After breakfast an attempt to wash and shave was made, arms were inspected and trenches tidied up and such repairs that could be carried out in daylight undertaken."[4]

Brian took over the command of Bowring's C company in the summer of 1915. One of the tasks was to build breastworks. These, constructed of sandbags, were to provide cover from rifle-fire. Brian enjoyed organising his men and setting up working parties that filled 2,000-4,000 sandbags a night. He was proud of his managerial skills and had occasion to remember Flanders a couple of years later when a fellow commander's company managed to fill a mere 300 bags in Mesopotamia. "He has no control over his men," Brian told his diary with contempt.

Brian was pleased when his German skills proved useful at Givenchy. He was asked to read captured German officers' letters and make extracts of anything interesting. His German childhood had in no way affected his loyalties. He never held Germans in high regard, thought that they "just had no conception of the accuracy and weight of British musketry, so immeasurably superior to theirs." In general, he thought "the Germans are excellent in making plans – up to a point. They see the situation from their own point of view only. They lack the imagination to consider what the enemy might do, particularly an enemy like our Infantry."

Having suffered from influenza in April (and spent ten days in hospital) and from defective vision in August, Brian was seriously wounded at Loos on 26 September 1915. By that time he had been promoted to lieutenant and awarded the acting rank of captain. In hospital he may have regretted the loss of company command and acting rank but, being an optimist, he looked back in a positive fashion regardless: "My nine months with the Regiment in this campaign in Flanders had been happy. I never lost the sense of pride that, after all, I was privileged so to serve, of gay comradeship with Officers and Men and other Units, and of high adventure."

War brought fear. "I had often been afraid in Flanders. Who had not? I'll tell the man who says that he enjoyed shelling, that he's either a liar or a lunatic. Apart from occasional physical terror and the dejected sinking of the heart under protracted heavy shelling I had the fear that I'd get killed and leave her, my "Booshy" [pet name for Claire], alone, desolate and unprotected. I was fighting for my Beloved as well as for my King and Country – and her case was the most precarious."

There is no reason to assume that Brian still remembered Hans Blunck, his school friend from Hamburg. Blunck, by contrast, remembered Brian when he came to write his memoirs. He described how a shiver had gone down his spine when the boys said good-bye to each other. Aged about twenty, they had just completed their gymnasium studies and Brian was preparing to leave Hamburg for England. He turned to Blunck, "precocious and solemn", and predicted: "It is possible that one day there will be a war between us. I fear that we shall be fighting one another." Blunck, writing this many years later, had lost touch with his friend, but he did wonder: "Perhaps in the world war we really did stand against one another, perhaps he fell on the other side?"[5]

In fact Brian was badly wounded in the chest, as a German bullet went through his left lung. "My life was saved entirely by my charging (on the 26th) at the Quarries at Hulluch, running so fast, so bold-headed, that I was leaning well forward, when a bullet hit me well below the left collarbone. It struck obliquely down, missing the heart by less than an inch and the aorta by a mere fraction and came out below the left shoulder-blade. Virtue rewarded!" Nearly half of the 2nd battalion were put out of action – 13 officers, four of them killed, and over 300 NCOs and men. Only at nightfall, amid pouring rain, was it possible to collect the wounded and count the losses.[6]

Brian was sent to England to convalesce. He was at Howard Home in Brighton where in summer 1916 he had tubercular glands removed, only to find that a week later a new crop appeared that had to be removed. He had a total of four operations for the glands and even years later there was a scar on the right side of his neck. "By then it was summer, and I started playing golf on the glorious links on the downs, with little skill but great zest. That vigorous exercise, and the Brighton sea air, did the rest, and in September I returned to duty as fit as flea," he said. "I had at last recovered – mainly thanks to golf, which I played very badly but the wonderful joy and exhilaration of which on the glorious Brighton course I still remember with gratitude to God – and returned to Light

Duty in October." Light duty meant a posting to Fort Tregantle in Cornwall where Barton, a fellow officer, was pleased to play beginners' golf with him. Barton has described Tregantle as a beautiful place, lonely and perched on the cliffs overlooking the white sands of Whitsand Bay.

At Tregantle Brian assisted his friend, Capt Frank Stacke, in charge of a field training company. Stacke, however, soon left, recommending that Brian should succeed him in command. Brian enjoyed the commanding job immensely. He was also good at instruction. Fond of organising most things, he lovingly listed the areas of instruction he was involved in: "Artillery Formations. Advance in Sections. Extended Lines. Fire and Movement. Use of Cover. Digging small trenches. Revetting and repairing trenches. Standing To, and so on and so forth."

13. Capt H. FitzMaurice Stacke whom Brian called Frank.

Courtesy of Mercian Regiment Museum (Worcestershire).

An Irish Catholic, highly intelligent but pessimistic in outlook, Stacke was a good friend. "He may have thought that I had brains of a sort and often warned me that the English did not like clever people – they were suspicious of them," Brian wrote later, suggesting that he was perceived as an outsider by some. "He did more for me than I can say, fathering me in the Regiment from the time of my attachment, bringing me up in its glorious traditions and those of the glories, and requirements, of the British Army generally, and often lending me money.

He knew well however that there were many blind spots and indeed severe gaps in my mental make-up." Stacke gave Brian books and Brian very much appreciated these gifts. There was a Rupert Brook and Voltaire's *Candide*. Stacke said that Brian resembled the protagonist of Voltaire's novel. (Candide is a naive young man who maintains his optimism despite various calamities that befall him.)

Claire came for a visit while Brian was at Tregantle and this was a happy time for the couple. A year later, when ill with sandfly fever in Mesopotamia, Brian recalled Tregantle. Almost delirious, filled with remorse and worry, he wrote page after page about his love affair with Billie and how this had affected Claire. Brian was convalescing in Brighton in 1915-16 when he fell in love with Billie, a small, fair-haired American girl with a "southern" voice. Even in 1917, feverishly agonising, Brian wrote that "excepting Claire I love Billie more than any woman I have ever met." Claire found out about the affair thanks to unspecified "stupidity" on Brian's part. Having just delivered their stillborn baby, she arrived in Brighton and demanded that Billie leave, then relented and graciously allowed the lovers to spend a final day together.

Remorseful, Brian still insisted in Mesopotamia: "God knows I don't want to forget [Billie]. The memory of our complete, carefree happiness, of our sad, tearful parting – and the bitter longing." Equally intensely Brian felt that "with all my love for Billie I never forgot Claire for an hour – and with my decidedly unconventional ideas on morals it never struck me that I was in any way doing Claire wrong. I just accepted Billie as a special happiness given me by the Gods, as if they had sent me a *real* little nymph, suddenly incorporated for my special benefit." At some point it dawned on Brian that he had "offended Claire, my Booshy, my little missis, whom I'd sworn to love, protect and cherish, and hurt her most awfully. She put her foot down, and loyal to the last, Billie left Brighton. It never occurred to her to refuse – she just dried her tears and left."

Brian's feverish ramblings fail to clarify the sequence of events. Claire was once very ill and nearly died. Was that before or after the stillbirth? Was her illness brought on by her husband's infidelity? Brian just insisted: "I loved [Claire] so very, very dearly all the time, yet when she needed me most, I found it in my heart to love Billie as well – when she most wanted me, all to herself, I was happy without her, with Billie and others, at Brighton... I did not realise that I was hurting her... And when God gave her back to me, in spite of all my sin, and she still loved me, although I hurt her so, I do think I wasn't always as really good to her as I might have been." Notice the ease with which Brian slipped in the words "and others". Elsewhere he has referred to his "other sentimental friendships or flirtations and little peccadilloes."

Chapter 3

Heat and dust of Mesopotamia

By January 1917 Brian was apparently strong enough for a long voyage, if not yet fit for battle: he was sent to southern India. His instruction skills at Tregantle had passed muster, so for a few months he trained NCOs in Belgaum. In May he was declared completely recovered and was ordered to join his 9th battalion. This involved more travel because the battalion had meanwhile gone to Mesopotamia. There had been bitter fighting and heavy losses but now, having pushed the Turks further and further north, the men were resting at a camp near Baqubah. By the time Brian joined them, fighting in the area had stopped and Mesopotamia had become a sideshow.

Brian started a diary in Bombay. This is where he embarked on the voyage to Mesopotamia. It is the only diary of his to survive. The bound black book covers a period of two months. About half of it is about the joys of travel, the second half is about camp life. There are daily entries, about the passing scenery, the books he was reading, officers he was talking to, but there was plenty of space for reflection. Claire was frequently in his thoughts, more often than not in connection with anxiety and guilt.

About a thousand men of various regiments were on board the HMT Ellenga at Bombay, bound for Mesopotamia.

"This is really the nearest approach to yachting on a large scale imaginable," Brian said, enjoying the ease and comfort of the ship. "The physical training we do with the men just helps to keep us fit, CO's rounds – at 11 – to remind us that we are soldiers. For the rest we have a topping crowd, glorious quarters, scrumptious meals, iced drinks, pleasant bridge and an all-round ripping time." There were quiet periods: "I spent the early afternoon writing and reading and listening to the droning of the wind, which I love," he wrote one day. Bridge occupied many an enjoyable hour. Always money conscious, Brian noted that "cards have provided a pleasant and useful addition to my pay." One good morning started with "late and satisfying tea", followed by "a topping bath, shave, hairbrush etc on deck in a clean suit of pyjamas and my scarlet silk dressing gown with white facings which I've had ever since my second year at Oxford."

Always a natty dresser, Brian instructed his servant, Jarman, to help him with his clothes. "I'm afraid the good Jarman is rather an ass," he complained. "It isn't only that he has lost my water-bottle, but also the matter of my shirts. I have four, or had four really good-looking shirts – one white, and three yellow ones, one of the latter with a torn sleeve which I told him to mend. I also had three khaki cotton shirts which he appears to have lost and of one of which I told him to make shoulder-straps for the good-looking ones. To-day he came to me with a pleased grin on his ugly features, carrying, waving one of my priceless canaries in about six pieces – 'I've ripped this one up proper for shoulder-straps, Sir.'"

Jarman alternately amused and irritated Brian. The servant soon managed to lose Brian's walking stick and this really annoyed Brian because it had been a gift from Claire. Brian had enthusiastically carved "GYFF-HYS-STICKE" on it. Whenever he used it, he thought of Claire. And now it was lost. Not that Brian had failed to instruct the servant: "I had told him how much store I set by it, that I prized it more than anything else I possessed," Brian lamented.

On another occasion, however, Brian was much amused by the servant. "I don't think I've done old Jarman full justice. He is the most absolutely preposterous servant I have met and deserves a book to himself. A rambling, discursive and comfortable talker when given full rein, he gets his eye-teeth well forward, and talks, mainly through the nose, browsing and ruminating aloud on many things. Yesterday he gave Carter and me a disquisition, rambling and wandering off into many side-tracks, but very exhaustive, on lock making, and lock and safe breaking. He has a very poor opinion of burglars and could give them many a hint. In fact, if he cared to – and he almost smiled. He has served me badly, but tenderly."

Brian took his duties on board the Ellenga seriously. He loved food and was therefore, quite appropriately, appointed officer in charge of the galley. In this enjoyable position he, however, discovered serious shortages (notably 3 ¾ lbs of tobacco and thirteen bottles of vinegar). A quantity of tinned salmon had gone off and had to be thrown away. Brian diligently copied some ledger details into his diary, proud of his record keeping, for which he received fulsome praise at the destination. This delighted him, but he was even more delighted with the net profit he had managed to make. "What pleases me," Brian noted, "is that I made the contractor pay for his putrid stuff and deficiencies instead of the soldiers, the Government, or I paying, and that I credited him with the over-issue of 100 cheroots – baksheesh, I suppose. I also made a note of the fact that the 5 tins [of] pineapple, not shown in invoice, were issued to fatigue parties."

Apart from the herrings in tomato sauce that disagreed with him, Brian has unfortunately described no other food eaten on board, although he repeatedly said that the food was good. As if to make up for this lack of detail, he listed the provisions purchased on arrival in the wonderful town of Ashar whence the men were going to journey upstream: "Tinned fruit, tongue, sausages, baked beans, other vegetables and food, Ideal Milk, porridge, jam, biscuits, acid drops, whiskey, lime juice, potted meat, cigarettes, cheroots, matches, a soap-dish, vaseline, quinine, hair tonic, rear-bumf, a tie-pin, a fly-flapper." Brian liked making lists. He also liked Ashar, then and on a later visit. "This is the scene of Arabian nights," he enthused. "I've always liked Ashar tremendously and found it truly oriental – you make your way through narrow alleys, high brick-built houses with shuttered wooden balconies on either side, through with all the people of the East and West, veiled women in black, some carrying pitchers on their heads, fierce, mitred long-haired Persians, here and there strings of donkeys."

14. British soldiers watching local people in Ashar (Basra), 1918.

A paddle steamer took the men from Basra to Baghdad. Brian was proud to be made the adjutant of the boat. "I'm practically running the show and thoroughly enjoy organizing it and getting everything as smart as possible," he said eagerly. Mesopotamia was hot, very hot, and full of insects. "I hate creepy, crawly things," Brian said. "Had a frightful lot of insects in the saloon during and after dinner. They kept getting into the soup and drinks – it was a race between them and us for the former, and the drinks have to be covered over as soon as they're poured out." A bridge session was practically ruined. "The last part of the evening was rather interfered with by positively amazing bugs and insects and really incredible numbers – hundreds of small grey and large black scarabs, an even larger kind called the *bourdon* from the deep hum of his flight, scores of filthy 'flying ants', dozens of other moths, beetles etc., five or six 'praying mantes', and finally a sort of flying crab or lobster, about five inches long, with claws and wings. That finished me, and I very soon after made a bee-line for my bed and the inside of my mosquito net."

Recent battles had left their mark on the landscape. "We passed a Turkish gun-boat our people had sunk, and several boats the Turks themselves had scuttled to bar the fairway." Further upstream, on a river bend at Kut, a scene of bitter fighting and heavy losses, Brian was delighted to see the Union Jack flying. "Most of the town is not as badly touched by shell-fire as towns and villages in France where there has been any fighting. The Northern end has been pretty badly knocked about, a big mosque partly destroyed, and the liquorice factory on the right bank looks very much like the same sort of thing in France – a bit of wall, a boiler, and a lot of twisted iron. One's feelings were mixed of pride, sympathy, resolve, and awe – but you can't gas about that sort of thing."

War regulations meant that the loss of even a single rifle was a serious matter. The entire ship was searched when one of the men claimed to have lost his; it had allegedly fallen overboard. Brian explained: "In any case the matter is out of our hands as the man will have to be remanded for a Court-Martial – the iron rule in case a rifle is lost in Mesopotamia or even India. This stringent rule is due to the fact that hundreds of rifles have been stolen by Arabs right under the noses of sentries, and in spite of the fact that men would sleep on their rifles buried in niches in the ground. The thief would simply cut the man's throat and get away with the rifle. At Amara last year Arabs got into a camp of two battalions, through a deep wire entanglement and a dense cordon of sentries, cut the throats of a number of men, and got away with 23 rifles, scot free."

Brian's diary is sprinkled with short prayers – "without prayer I cannot live," he wrote. Sometimes they are for Claire, sometimes in search of general guidance: "O God – turn this trial to the best effect. Grant me certain Faith and Hope, knowledge of Thee – of Truth – of what I should do. Teach me to worship Thee and the Gods who serve Thee in due proportion. Let me leave the earth a better place, and others happier. Do a miracle and give me certainty of faith. Amen."

Church was important in wartime. One Sunday only fifteen men turned up for a service and some were in their shirtsleeves. Brian was annoyed. He ordered the men to fetch their coats and the missing fellows, then apologised to the padre. The men's slowness exasperated him. "I went below, and by Jove, lightning and thunder played about in those two decks, according to the best Bowring tradition. Among other telling bits I told them they'd be damned glad of a service when half of them had been killed and the remainder down with all the diseases of Mesopotamia, writhing with dysentery and raving and gasping with heatstroke."

In Basra "church parade was put in orders in the face of some opposition from the Major who wouldn't take it and expected it to be a failure, as we had neither books nor music. But all officers rolled up and sang like larks, the deck was crowded, Cpl Sutcliffe gave the pitch, I made the Service (my fourth) shorter than the usual even – leaving out the Venite – and selected three well-known hymns, all of which went well, particularly 'Onward, Christian Soldiers' which went gloriously."

War had decimated the ranks; good men were in short supply. This translated into good news for Brian: "They've made me a Brigadier – unfortunately without acting rank, pay, allowances, red tabs, brass hat and the rest of it – in fact OC 39th Bde details." Brian revelled in his promotion and looked forward to new responsibilities. At a camp near Baghdad, when told of his shared command of a draft of 740 men on the following morning, he took it in his stride. This left a whole evening ahead; he and his companions seized the opportunity to explore Baghdad, the town he was to return to more than once. However, the magic of Ashar was not to be repeated. "Our first impressions of Baghdad were this steep dignity of the banks, a gleaming silver haze, the residency, now GH2, with the Union Jack flying, a lot of date-palms and, rising from the middle of the city, the beautiful azure cupola of a large mosque. Generally speaking the Town is full of life and colour, particularly the Bazaars, decidedly Eastern in character, and we found it extremely interesting – but dusty and without shade, flat, and without gardens, crowded, and empty of glamour. We did not feel the beauty and romance of the Orient here as at Ashar." Not a patch on Cairo or Constantinople, Brian concluded. This didn't prevent Brian and his companions from enjoying iced lime squashes and tea at the Hotel Maude that only recently had been occupied by pro-German officers.

15. A market in Ashar (Basra), 1920.

The next day's march to Childayah was a disaster. Some of the route was beautiful, along the river, but it was too hot and many men fell by the wayside. Brian didn't do badly: at one point he was even offered beer to drink, but for men there wasn't enough water. As the day wore on, all were struggling, despite stops. "On the subsequent march of about two miles two of my men fell out, I was carrying the rifles of two others and the rest dragged themselves into camp about 1.20 pm. Successive parties arrived, about 40 having been left in ambulances, the last arriving at 4 pm," Brian wrote when they reached the camp. Findon, who shared command of the draft, told Brian of the difficulties he had had with men from the Loyal North Lancashire Regiment: "they [were] simply falling out in dozens by the road-side where they would have stayed and lain all day. Bringing them along was like cattle-driving."

The camp was pleasant, in the shade of a palm grove, close to a river. "Bathing is not allowed," Brian wrote, "owing to the dangerous currents and whirlpools, only washing, knee-deep in the river. The men however enjoyed this immensely, and so did we, spending about an hour over a delicious sponge-bath."

However, Brian was angry that the march had been so badly organised. And it was just day one, with four more to go. It was beyond his comprehension "that men who have had no exercise at all, some for as much as 5 weeks, should be required to start the march with a 14-mile stage – the longest of the lot. Tomorrow's stage is only seven miles," he told his diary, listing the things that had gone wrong. They had started out late, missing the cool of the morning that would have made things easier, "no ambulance, Medical Officer or orderly went with the column" and "no drinking water beyond what the men carried in water-bottles was carried or provided on the way." He and Findon as commanders should have been mounted and given a decent map, he thought. "Before I turned in, I had a great spider-hunt. I *loathe* spiders and always have done, and Jarman and I killed 7 huge disgusting Jerry Mandalums between us."

The second marching day proved easier, particularly as Brian managed to get himself a pony, but on the third day he too succumbed to the sun and fell ill. His arrival at the camp was delayed by a week. He joined the battalion on 1 June, an auspicious date for the regiment, and was put in charge of D company. Pleased to command six officers, a warrant officer and 167 NCOs and men, Brian was uneasy about sidelining 2/Lt F.D. Drewitt, who had been in charge until then. "For me of course, having commanded my company in a Regular Battalion in France for four months in 1915, it isn't such a tremendous catch," Brian wrote, realising that Drewitt might be upset being his 2nd in command, but no longer in charge.

And indeed, a couple of weeks later, rivalries surfaced when Drewitt put in a complaint about favouritism. It was "the old-timer's jealousy against the new arrivals," as Brian logged it. "Of course I feel sorry for Drewitt," he said, "but what are his few months in Mesopotamia to, let us say, my five and half years [of] regular service and my year in France." If each man complained about his superior, Brian wondered, what would become of good fellowship and service in general. He called his men and told them that personal friendships did not interfere with the duty roster – this had been the gist of Drewitt's complaint. He hoped that his openness would put an end to the matter and it seemed to have worked. Something still rankled because Brian made no mention in his diary of the Military Cross that Drewitt had been awarded for his leadership at Kut – he had led a platoon in digging communications trenches under heavy Turkish fire.[1]

Brian was pleased with his men. They had been "mostly civilians to start with, now veterans – their temper is good, though they are not as cheery as they would be in a happier climate, the discipline is good and they pull together well."

During the next peaceful months the battalion stayed close to the so-called Sindiyah-Windiyah line in central Mesopotamia. It was a hot and dusty area where palms, mulberry and orange trees, but not much else grew. Brian liked the place. "The country is rather lovely – flat of course, but cut with banked nullahs [dry river-beds], covered with scrub, still green, and dotted with palm groves. It's particularly beautiful in the early morning and at night, when the earth takes on a richer hue, the palms seem to stand higher and deep blue-grey shadows rise and stand between them. The scrub seems to keep the dust down and we watch the sand-devils racing – sky-high – in the distance." Green bee-eaters darted about and this made Brian wax lyrical: "It was a glorious morning and a joy to be alive. The air at the break of day here is like strong wine, the sunlight like pure gold, a little breeze plays in the palm tops and the brushwood, the swallows who have come down during the last few days, are darting here and there. God's in His heaven, all's well with the world."

The battalion's task was to support and fortify the line of outposts. This meant digging, which was possible only in the cool hours of the morning. Brian, who listed military engineering among his many interests, drew comparisons. "These works are as per drillbook and so different from the trenches in France," he observed. "There the line was the result of opportunity and necessity – dug where we managed to hang on in retreat or were stopped and had to dig in – manholes scooped out with the entrenching tool and joined up later – its position dictated by the then tactical situation, its construction adapted to the weather conditions – improved and repaired by makeshift, altered and reconstructed as the ever changing situation allowed and demanded. Here an ideal line has been chosen by the GOC (with the Turk 20 to 30 miles away) running from river to river across open and perfectly level country, planned, drafted and designed by the DRE [detachment of royal engineers?] with consideration of its most final development and is being constructed under what are perfect and ideal conditions as long as working parties are confined to the cool of the morning and evening."

On the mornings when there was no working party, there was PT under platoon commanders. Sometimes Brian led the company in "extended order drill (on word of command) by platoons. Like all men who've ever been in action they think they know it all backwards, but though they're quite good a little practice won't do them any harm, going by what I've seen today."

The company enjoyed a living mascot, a big fat sheep called Billy. The barber, Huxley, had caught him when he was a little lamb. Used to the men and their routine, Billy

-63-

followed them like a dog. "The men set a tremendous store by him," Brian said. He acquired a personal pony whom he called Traveller after the animal owned by the American Gen Robert E. Lee. Traveller was good for polo practice. There were also opportunities, and time, for pleasure rides in the vast open spaces around the camp. "Out to No 4 Strong Point this morning on Traveller," Brian wrote enthusastically, "through the camel-scrub, then across the dry bed of the Narwhan-canal, picking our way through the network of water-courses, and a topping hand-gallop to finish up with. He is a handful, and I must get that martingale."

The pony rides improved Brian's singing voice. He may not have been a trained singer, which is what the KGB sources have suggested, but he certainly had a fine voice and good repertoire; he loved singing. "I find these rides through the wide open spaces in the cool morning breeze great for singing and my voice 100 pc better than ever before."

It was rare for the war to be heard – the camp location was remote. On occasion a Turkish aeroplane strayed overhead, to be met by British artillery fire. Unexpected excitement was caused by a raid on a June morning. "A party of about 50 or 60, probably Arab irregulars – for their rifles seemed various and their shooting damnable – had come down... and opened fire," Brian told his diary and wondered whether they were after the camp supplies. The raiders promptly fled once a Vickers gun came to life.

The biggest problem was water. For Brian, who with great enthusiasm described a canvas bath he enjoyed, this was close to tragedy. However, the level in the El Khalis canal went down and Brian observed: "The great trouble of the country is a lack of water. The Turks have dammed the Tawilah higher up – there are only a few inches of water in the Tawilah, and all the orange and pomegranate trees at Abu Tamar are dying. We are sending up an Arab party to cut the Turkish dam." Water for drinking and cooking at the camp was rationed; there was no water for washing until the camp moved.

Sandflies were tiny, but also constituted a big problem: a single bite might lead to a fever. The medical officer recommended an unorthodox prophylactic measure: the officers were to drink plenty of Cointreau, and that would impregnate the skin against the flies. The measure can't have worked because for a time Brian and Carter were the only officers still fit for work. Soon Brian developed a blister on his knee, which burst and went septic. "My sore is properly septic this morning and [I] only hope it won't spread. Beastly. I feel hot and tired. The temperature is 112 in the shade." This was Fahrenheit – 44 degrees Celsius – not at all unusual for a Mesopotamian summer. "The sick-rate, by the way, is positively alarming. Since I've come up here 24 have gone to hospital, mostly with sandfly, some with sun," Brian wrote just a month after his arrival at the camp.

Officers, on the whole, did not do badly. Brian had a clerk attached to him, and a servant, and he shared his tent with Capt G.E. Boshier, while his men slept eighteen to a tent. When beer was delivered the officers had a bottle each, while the men drew lots and some had to go without. "The winners, in a long queue, as pleased as children, and [I] have not seen a number of men so glad to be alive since I've been in this country. Real *joie de vivre*, real high spirits – really very touching," said Brian condescendingly.

More personal attention was to come. "I had a wire from Brigade, telling me that I'm OC Wing Worcs (B and D coys)," Brian wrote with pride, "and shall get my orders from 39th Brigade HQ direct. Top-hole job, on my own out here. Wish it would last for ever." Henceforth Brian was able to issue "Wing Orders". He lovingly copied a few of those in his diary. For most part they included words like "duties" and "reveille" and suggested an orderly camp routine. At the same time the men were told: "Should a hostile aeroplane bomb the encampment Garrisons of Lunettes will double into the trenches, D Coy will occupy neighbouring nullahs and keep down." Hard to believe that with a threat of a bomb hanging over them, a pay parade would be held, but it did: an officer arrived carrying cash (3,000 chips). Brian quite surprised him by insisting that the cash should be counted first. As Brian put it, "the regular soldier is brought up to be jolly careful where public money is concerned, and after all I've got to sign a receipt for the thing." And he was justified: the total was 500 chips short!

Brian hasn't explained what kind of chips. His diary references to bridge winnings and losses are inconsistent. Rupees mentioned on leaving India were soon replaced by chips (or chipps). "I have now, since leaving Belgaum, won 384 Rupees, having started with 9 in my pocket. I've paid all my exes, mess bills, tips, kit, stores for the Coy, had a damn good time and 150 chipps left, besides what old Findon owes me. Jolly good and shall send Booshy and the mater some," he wrote on 25 May. Sending money to England didn't seem to present problems.

Brian's diary records a dream he had: the king had been deposed and a republic declared. Not yet fully awake, he seized a pen and filled three pages in defence of monarchy. He started with recollections of 1910 when the Oxford University Officers' Training Corps that he had joined lined the road at Windsor for the funeral of King Edward VII. He went on to explain what monarchy stood for. "To have a King, a symbolic but human personality, one who is above party, the first of his peers, the true representative of the nation, the first gentleman of the country, one to give the lead in all things, one ultimately to be appealed to, one to express what the nation feels. To have a King is to have a thing we cannot do without. However I suppose the above is largely a matter of taste and opinion. Lots of people don't see and feel these things. It is however I think true that a monarchy provides a strong central government, an ordered administration, stability of institutions. All other forms of Government have led either to weakness, to anarchy, to the terrible tyranny of the many, of the few, or the despotism, sometimes benevolent, of the one strong egotist – not counting many other abuses."

On another occasion Brian gave full vent to his feelings when he picked up what he called "that poisonous rag *Truth*", a Melbourne-based newspaper, in which he spotted a "ghastly" article by Scrutator. Brian was outraged by Scrutator because his piece was "absolutely treasonable disloyalty. He refers to our Monarchy as an anachronism – in view of the Russian alliance and revolution and to our 'picturesque but antiquated military despotism'. Military Despotism! Our vascillating, mob-ridden democracy, jostling along behind the party caucus, in front a few inefficients like Asquith, more pushed than leading, ever treading delicately and pandering to the multitude lest they lose their coveted place and its emoluments. Apart the one symbol of dignity, permanence and central government, the focus of loyal sentiment and enthusiasm – the King. What would Scrutator give us instead? The tyranny of the demagogue and trades union? Or anarchy and graft. But that such treasonable piffle can be printed is indeed terrible." Brian knew where he and his men stood: "All of us on board [the Ellenga] of course are staunch loyalists."

At the Tawilah camp he was deeply upset to hear an Irishman, Craig, OC of B Company, say that he was "entirely in sympathy with the Sinn Feiners, that he was fighting not for the Empire but for Ireland and would fight for her against England *at least* as readily as against Germany, for which war this one would be 1st class experience." Brian thought this was treasonable. He was confident that "only a Monarchy, with Court and trappings, seems to me in the least compatible with the dignity of a great Sovereign Empire like ours."

Chapter 4

Travel and training years

Five months before the First World War ended Brian's battalion was granted leave to India. For several weeks Brian and friends roamed around, starting with Calcutta that was filled with "gorgeous scents and sights and an old-world atmosphere." There was the luxury of unlimited baths and a visit to a golf club. Dental appointments were made. The men had time to discuss their soldiering future. For the first time Brian mentioned the secret service. His friend Capt Stacke had left the regiment for intelligence.

16. The Candacraig Hotel, Maymyo, 2012.

Next they went to Burma which looked "a little like Cambridgeshire" to Brian. There was golf, tennis, ice cream, caviar sandwiches, snooker, dancing lessons, glorious fireflies and sweet, strong night-air at the hill station of Maymyo. At the Candacraig Hotel Brian invented a range of cocktails to honour the women he had known: "the Violet, Billie, Claire, Roma, Lizzie." The morning after was a "painful recovery from last night's events – glorious air and topping bath." Back in Calcutta, then Allahabad, "eating mangoes with a razor", then Bombay.

17. Interior of the Candacraig, 2012.

Having survived the hangovers of Burma and India with good grace, Brian fell ill on his return to Mesopotamia. He was hospitalised at Basra's Officers' Hospital No 3 BGH. This was where he heard the "glorious news" that his brigade had been dispatched to Persia. Once discharged from the hospital, he continued to travel north, in the direction of Persia, occasionally still suffering from a fever and taking quinine. Fascinated by bazaars, he visited one at Kut where he bought a "big heavy luscious luminous stone, in colour like a ruby, but lighter" and also a sapphire for Claire. A visit to friends of friends included "the most frumptious tea in Mesopotamia, with bread and butter, and a glorious iced cake, and coffee and vanilla ices."

Keeping his eyes and ears open for news, Brian observed that "the new show in France", with Douglas Haig in command, was going well and "the Russian counter-revolution seems to be doing well." Having mourned the loss of seven chips at bridge, he focused on the harrowing tale a British officer had brought back from Persia. "He told us that the famine in Persia is truly awful – men, women and children dying of hunger by the roadside, dying by inches, too weak to drag themselves out of the road. He says the indifference of the natives to each other's suffering is horrible – we can do so little, being short of rations which are hard to get up – in fact have to rely in part on local purchase so that – good God – we can't help taking more food out of the country – it's simply dreadful and thinking that I'll have to see it all and be powerless to help has made the taste of this glorious adventure bitter in my mouth. The Russians, undisciplined swine, had raped, robbed and burnt everything. Now the crops have failed and the Persian Government is hopelessly indifferent and ineffective. He says he saw some corpses who were just skeletons. Oh, curse the war – curse the Huns. I shall put up one third my ration and shall get my subalterns and volunteers in the company to do the same." On the broader war scene Brian sounded defiant: "The Boche gets caught out every time by thinking we haven't a kick left in us when we have."

From August Brian was in beautiful northwestern Persia where for a few months he was "on special duty". In Kermanshah he was ordered to investigate the constant interruptions on the telegraph line with Hamadan. Col A.M. Moras in a letter to 9th Worcestershire has confirmed that Brian "was employed on this duty from September 17th to September 26th. He carried out his mission very satisfactorily and showed great keenness in the performance of his difficult duties. The results of his investigation on paper may have seemed disappointing to him, but the negative information that he gained that there were no agents among the Jelu refugees proved most valuable." The Jelu were a tribe fleeing from Turkish persecution who had set up camp in Persia.

Having rejoined his battalion in the coastal town of Resht, Brian was sent further north, into the Caucasus. This was an area of ethnic and political complexities, afflicted with restlessness and demands for independence. Turkey had taken advantage of the confusion and occupied the land around Baku for its oil. However, an armistice was signed and the Turks agreed to withdraw. Brian in Baku was part of the British peacekeeping force whose job it was to supervise the Turkish troop withdrawal. The British were expected to administer justice, conciliate the warring inhabitants and organise supplies. Food riots were a frequent occurrence, the British troops were small and dispersed, not strong enough to deal with any serious uprising.

No wonder that Brian was utterly exhausted in April 1919 when the British left Baku. There was also the frustration that the local Azeri people, having got rid of the Turks, failed to assert their independence: it was the Bolshevik rule that won. When Brian arrived at Stetchworth on home leave, he was craving peace and quiet, but found turmoil instead. His wife "Claire had cast me off and was now living in her lover's flat in London," Brian wrote later. Helena, Brian's mother, was welcoming but elderly. She was still, just, the proud owner of The Firs, but was now aged 74. The local vicar, Alfred Burton, who had married Brian and Claire, was concerned that Helena might not be able to look properly after the war-weary soldier. He and Mrs Burton invited Brian to share their lunches and Brian gratefully accepted.

The lunch arrangement led Brian to another of his love affairs. It was one of the vicar's daughters, Margaret Burton, who offered him "love and friendship". Brian, 5 foot 9½ and of slight build, was physically very weak, very much in need of care and attention. "I had had malaria round about Christmas 1918," he wrote, "and had almost died of Spanish influenza in Baku and needed feeding up and sympathy and love and I got it all in full measure from her – dear Margaret." She, like all his other women, inspired him to compose love poems.

The affair with Margaret helped Brian to recover. His home leave lasted for four months, sufficiently long for recuperation. As soon as he could, however, he applied to go back to Russia. In Baku he had for the first time heard Russian spoken and he was hooked. On the lookout for new passions, the language fascinated him. Brian and Lt J.R.W. King were the only two officers from the Worcestershire Regiment to join the British military mission to south Russia.

While waiting to hear, Brian stayed in London, helping his friend Capt Stacke, who was writing a regimental history. "For a few weeks after the war I worked with him at Whitehall Gardens on the History of the War until I got my wish and got out to Gen Briggs's – by then Gen Holman's – Military Mission to South Russia," Brian recalled.

It was not only the south of Russia that was in turmoil; there was chaos across the country. The October revolution of 1917 had destroyed the old certainties. The old empire was pulling at the seams everywhere. The countries on the Baltic, for example, were lucky: Finland proclaimed its independence in December 1917, Estonia and Lithuania followed in February 1918 and Latvia, in November 1918. These former tsarist provinces were not, however, strong enough to fight back the advancing Bolshevik troops, keen to achieve a world revolution. Allied help was sought. In the Baltic it was Gen Nikolai Yudenich and in the south, Gen Anton Denikin, who invited the British to assist, and intervention fitted in with British interests.

Small British missions were sent. Meanwhile expectations were high. "The Civil War could not last long now as the army that had recently defeated the mighty Germans would have no trouble at all defeating the Bolshevik riff-raff. On the other side of the frontline the Bolshevik units were shocked by the arrival of the British and started to send alarming reports to their headquarters and to Moscow."[1]

Only a couple of months before Brian's arrival in southern Russia there was much military progress to report from the area that falls into today's Ukraine or is just outside. "Along the whole front from the Caspian to the Sea of Azov, four Red armies have been thoroughly defeated, have lost half their number, and are still retreating. General Denikin's forces have captured 22,000 prisoners, 150 guns, 350 machine-guns, four armoured trains, and an immense quantity of other booty," a London newspaper said.[2] Another reported from the town of Poltava after the Bolsheviks had fled. "The meeting was held in the hall of the Nobles' Assembly, which the day previously was evacuated by the Bolshevist Soviet. In the big gilt frames where formerly hung the portraits of marshals of nobility there hung the tattered remains of the portraits of Lenin and Trotsky, and other Commissaries, hastily torn out before the meeting. There was something strangely sad, touching, and ghostly about the whole proceeding, like the shadowy resurrection from the dead of old days described by Turgenieff."[3]

By the time Brian arrived on the scene the victorious tide was over. He reported for duty on 2 October 1919 and straight away witnessed much brutality, suffering, confusion and fear. He was so shocked by what he had seen that he wrote a long letter to Claire in England. Torn between his duties as a soldier and a human being, Brian asked her to do "war work" with her typewriter "in doing the Bolshevist harm", as he put it.

In his letter Brian explained how the Bolsheviks had come to power and how the White commander, Denikin, was fighting for a united Russia. He then described the atrocities that had been photographed after the Bolshevik withdrawal from Odessa on the Black Sea. Most of the victims pictured were women with either breasts cut off or bodies sliced open – not the kind any newspaper would print. "They show men who've been crucified with the torture of the 'human glove'," Brian said. "The victim gets crucified, nails through his elbows. The hands are treated with a solution which shrivels the skin. The skin is cut out with a razor, round the wrist, and peeled off, till it hangs by the finger nails – the 'human glove'."

"I want you to put heart and soul into helping General Denikin and his cause," he told Claire, and asked her to pass the letter on to his friend Capt Stacke, who in turn gave it to *The Times*. Published anonymously on 14 November 1919, it was entitled "The horrors of Bolshevism". The paper felt it necessary to add a warning: "We make no apology in present circumstances for publishing certain passages of a nature generally considered 'unprintable'", and published Brian's letter in full.

Brian's hope was that his letter would "set England blazing with indignation and disgust" and there was indeed a huge reader response. The interest was such that *The Times* decided to reprint it as a pamphlet (a single copy sold at 1d. and 1,000 copies at three guineas). The paper also published responses from men who had recently visited the south of Russia, confirmed Bolshevik brutality and told the readers of their experience.

Brian was grateful that the paper's editor, Henry Wickham Steed, did not divulge his name to the prime minister's office, although there had been pressure for this from Number 10. Stories were circulating about David Lloyd George and a major-general who had had the temerity to contradict the prime minister about the number of British troops in Mesopotamia. The major-general was never employed again. Brian wondered what fate would have befallen him had Steed revealed his name, but concluded that "I should never have reached even the modest rank of Lt Col if he had given me away."

Over the nine months Brian spent in south Russia he saw town after town – Rostov, Novorossiisk, Taganrog, Novocherkassk – fall to the Bolsheviks.[4] The fall of Odessa in February 1920 was a turning point in the war. Brian, a liaison officer, was helping the Whites and their families to evacuate; there was no longer any hope of victory. The Allied intervention had failed, and not just in the south. On the other hand, the nations on the Baltic littoral were happy with the outcome of the civil war, grateful to the British for support for their independence. Estonia, Latvia and Lithuania each fought a war of independence and emerged victorious.

Maj-Gen Holman, commander of the British mission in south Russia, filed his final report in which he mentioned "the incompetence and corruption of the administrative services and departments" and referred to "a perpetual struggle to get things done". His operations were much hampered by the persistent rumours that the Allies were about to abscond and abandon the local population. Such talk had been going on for months and finally turned out to be true. After the British departure many local people faced Bolshevik reprisals.

Holman reported that a total of sixteen British officers and 29 other ranks were killed between October 1918 and March 1920; 736 were hospitalised (a large proportion, 266, for venereal disease).[5] Holman's report makes no mention of officers held captive, but Brian's regimental records say that he was "temporarily arrested" by the Bolsheviks.

Brian's experience of southern Russia didn't seem to dampen his spirits. Even when ill with jaundice and hospitalised in Istanbul, he retained his optimism and sense of humour. Jaundice inspired him to dedicate a poem to a fellow sufferer called Hugo:

"I watch you sitting on your bed
Opposite mine, with indigestion glum,
Your face, once tanned a healthy red,
Just like a lemon. Oh, you do look rum!
Hugo – poor, dear, old fellow
It makes me laugh to see you look so yellow.
Mind you, I realize that I myself perhaps
Might give the thoughtless reason for a titter,
But then – why should I want to look like other chaps?
If only my inside were quiet, and my tongue not quite so bitter
I wouldn't miss this show for any money
For really, Hugo, we look very funny."

Back with his regiment in England, Ireland and Germany, for Brian Russia faded into the background for several years. During this time Brian qualified as 1st class interpreter in

German and attended a number of courses to improve his army skills. "Altogether I succeeded in obtaining a 'Distinguished' certificate at three Army Educational Establishments: 1) at the School of Military Administration at Chiseldon in Wiltshire, after 3 months in autumn 1922, 2) in the 'Long', i.e. Ten-week course at the Small Arms School at Hythe in Jan or Feb to April 1924, and 3) at the Machine Gun at Netheravon ending in the late autumn of 1926. Three 'D's on 'Long' Courses must have been a rave, if not unique achievement." Among the courses "the most enjoyable and profitable to me of all [was] a Fencing Course (including training in the Scots Sword dance) and, in my last year as Adjutant, an Adjutants' Physical Training Course at the PT School at Aldershot."

Brian had been the adjutant with the 3rd City of London Regiment, Territorial Force. "From July 1923 to Sept 1926 (incl) I only took 10 days leave once, for the rest I put myself on every course I could get hold of," he said proudly.

The machine-gun course was something special inasmuch as he did not choose it himself. It was Lt-Col F.P. Dunlop, commander of the 2nd battalion, who recommended it. Dunlop had taken an interest in Brian and invited him and his wife to a London hotel for dinner. "Claire was still my wife, though by name only, but we were great friends," Brian said in comment. The dinner was an enjoyable occasion, but there was more to follow. "Over the coffee, if not before, Col Dunlop told me that heavier Infantry armament and mechanised transport were to be expected. The Machine Gun Platoon of four Vickers MGs would be expanded into a MG Company of eight guns (with a view of a final war establishment of 16 guns in 4 sections). Would I like to take it? It quite took my breath away. Of course I said that I should love it, but equally naturally that I knew nothing about machine guns. That, said Dunlop, would not

18. Capt C.K.O.B. Giffey's military travel permit, 1926.

matter – if I would take it on he would send me on a Long Course at the MG School at Netheravon."

Brian was delighted. The course at Netheravon was "most important" because it supplemented what he had already learnt at Chiseldon and Hythe and, additionally, taught him tactics. "Netheravon did more for me even than that. It gave me confidence. I learnt to give my opinion and to stick to it, with assurance. And even more than that: I learnt more about people than ever before." There were 32 on the course, most of them interesting and delightful people.

Having "learnt to drive a four-horse MG Limber" at Netheravon, Brian "entered for the Rhine Army limber driving competition" in Wiesbaden and won. He was now part of the German Army on the Rhine. The regimental history has recorded that "for the Battalion perhaps the significance of training in Germany lay in the fact that it enabled the foundations of a great musketry tradition to be rebuilt. Competition shooting began. Teams were sent to Bisley which won the Roupell Cup and tied for the Small Arms Trophy."[6]

Brian had a long-standing interest in guns. At the ordnance store in Ashar, Mesopotamia, he had spotted "a topping long-barrelled Webley revolver, almost as good as the one I had to leave behind in the shell-hole when I had been wounded in the Loos show. I simply love a revolver and am a fair shot," he told his diary. In the 1920s, while with the 3rd London Regiment, he regularly attended Bisley. He was in the Army Revolver Thirty for five years and took part in the King's Prize, a magnificent competition, he said, involving rapid fire from ever decreasing distances. "The strongest contingents were musketry instructors, and I met my friend Staff-Sergeant Instructor Maltham again. I really owed my success at the Small Arms School at Hythe, and in a way at the MG School at Netheravon as well, to him. For in private lessons from him I had, by endless practice on an infinite variety of targets, and bitter perseverance, mastered the difficult task of the easy, quick and clear indication of targets, which, to start with, I had found terribly difficult – fire order and to give the best order quickly and clearly – without a moment's hesitation."

All this extra training and courses led to hopes of promotion. Col Dunlop, who thought highly of Brian, recommended him for accelerated promotion in 1927. It is interesting that Dunlop felt it necessary to add comments to say that Brian's "methods are somewhat unconventional, and he approaches his problems from a somewhat different angle from the average Infantry Officer", as if to justify his recommendation. Dunlop's summing up also laid an emphasis on Brian being different: "This officer is an unconventional type, and takes a certain amount of understanding. He has, however, produced very remarkable results, and has shown that he can impart his knowledge and energy to others... Can be relied on to forget nothing and omit nothing." Much to Brian's chagrin, accelerated promotion to major was not awarded.

Edward Barton of the Worcestershire Regiment has also mentioned Brian's unconventional, "broader outlook". He told the story of two dispatch riders arriving at Bethune in 1915 and Brian inviting them to share his table. "At that time for officers

19. Col F.P. Dunlop.
Courtesy of Mercian Regiment Museum (Worcestershire).

and other ranks to sit down together was unheard of," Barton remarked.[7] Was this to Brian's credit or might he have drawn criticism for his egalitarian views?

Having failed to gain promotion, Brian's thoughts returned to the Russian language. He had met Roman, a Russian speaker living in Riga, whose friendship encouraged him to change course. While nominally still with his regiment in Bingen in 1927, Brian spent three months in Riga. The Latvian capital suited him: it was very much like Bingen or Hamburg, with Germanic architecture and way of life, and yet different. Brian learnt that it had been the Archbishop of Hamburg-Bremen who in the 13th century had sent his nephew, Bishop Albert von Buxhoevede, to convert Latvia and Estonia to Christianity. Descendants of the medieval crusaders settled in the Baltic lands to govern them for centuries, up until the 1918 independence. German was still widely spoken and understood in the 1920s and 1930s.

It was in Riga that Brian embarked on a Russian course. It took him the best part of a year to master the language. It was time for a change. He loved his regiment, but he had heard that the British Army of the Rhine was about to be wound up. Army life was good, but he knew it inside out, having served in the Worcestershire Regiment for nearly 17 years. Furthermore, under the Foreign Office his link with his regiment was not to be severed, merely loosened.

Chapter 5

Secret agent in Tallinn

Brian joined MI6, the Secret Intelligence Service, in 1928 when he was 41 years old. "I have always looked upon life as a glorious adventure," he once remarked. Now he embarked on his new career with characteristic enthusiasm. Lloyds Bank was more down-to-earth when it sent him a standard letter: "Dear Sir, We have been advised by the War Office that you have been selected for appointment under the Foreign Office and pending further instructions regarding date of appointment your pay as from the 1st October becomes issuable in arrear."[1]

What constituted Brian's "selection" is not known, but Arthur Leslie Nicholson, who joined MI6 two years later, has explained what happened in his case. He had similarly been in army service in Germany. While on leave in London, Nicholson contacted military intelligence to enquire about a possible job. "As a result of this chance telephone call, I met a 'plain clothes' intelligence man and, after several meetings, he suggested that I resign my commission and enter a new field. I remember being a bit surprised and blurting out something about lack of experience. I soon discovered that my friend was as well-informed on this as I was: I had been fairly thoroughly investigated."[2] Nicholson was duly appointed, first to Prague, in 1930, and then to Riga, in 1934.

Brian's first posting as passport control officer took him to Estonia in January 1929. New to intelligence, he felt at home in Tallinn whose Germanic architecture and way of life reminded him of Riga and Bingen that he was familiar with. As to his work, he was expected to be "under instruction of Capt A. Ross."[3] Alexander Ross was one of Brian's predecessors in Tallinn.

20. Viru Gate in central Tallinn in the 1930s.

The idea of passport control officers had been operating since 1919 when the system was set up to gather intelligence on Bolshevik subversion. Soviet Russia remained the main target well into the 1930s. "Even when Anglo-Soviet diplomatic relations were established in 1924, Moscow remained too hostile an environment for a secure SIS station. SIS Soviet operations were conducted instead from states on Russia's borders, especially from Finland and the Baltic states."[4] Brian's main job was to keep an eye on Russia while ostensibly issuing visas and passports. There was a lot of passing traffic.

Brian put much effort into improving his Russian, practically living in the language during his first years in Tallinn. One of his duties was the routine perusal of Soviet industrial and military publications obtained with the help of the Estonian embassy in Moscow. These were hard to come by without Estonian help, but often contained valuable information. The official MI6 history says that Tallinn focused on military intelligence, Helsinki looked after naval matters and Riga took on political and economic targets, while Tallinn also played a coordinating role.[5]

At first Brian lived in the house of Peter Baranov, a Russian emigre, at Toompea (Kohtu 10) where he practised his newly-acquired Russian. The substantial Baranov house, close to the seat of the Estonian government and parliament, was always full of people, some of whom "came and went like the characters in a Dostoyevskian novel," a visiting American observed. "Also of interest were Baranov's boarders, half a dozen British Army and Navy Russian students who lent a Slavified Oxford-cum-vodka atmosphere."[6]

A somewhat similar atmosphere was a few years later observed by the writer Graham Greene on his visit to Tallinn. Greene ran into Peter Leslie, the vice-consul, and they had dinner together. "It's all amazingly cheap here," Greene told his wife in May 1934. "We had for dinner, the two of us, 6 vodkas, a delicious hors d'oeuvres, a Vienna schnitzel with fried potatoes, & two glasses of tea. Total bill in one of the swell restaurants 3/6d." Sleepy after the vodkas, Greene added: "I'm leaving the night life for Major Giffey to show me. He is the standing joke here, as the hearty fellow, hard drinker, man-about-Tallinn."[7] Brian had by then moved out of Baranov's residence to a flat in Hollandi põik. What Greene and Brian did together has not been described, but Greene's experience of Tallinn must have been memorable.

Greene even intended to set a novel in Tallinn (Our Man in Tallinn, instead of Havana) and he modelled a character, Captain Gullie, in another novel, *England Made Me*, on Brian. It was published in 1935, its action set largely in Stockholm.[8] Gullie is an episodic character, the British military attaché proud of his Scottish ancestry. He is a card player who smokes and drinks, has a ginger moustache, a monocle and a German mother. He likes to play pranks, paint ships, browse nudist magazines and wants to stage *The Mikado* and *Merrie England*. In a controversy he turns into an inoffensive pacifier – all in all a mild and rather silly caricature of Brian Giffey.

Brian had to face difficult realities in Estonia which in the early 1930s still behaved awkwardly, like a new country. Barely a year after his arrival Maj-Gen Johan Unt, commander of Tallinn garrison, was assassinated and his subsequent death caused a stir. Unt had been responsible for the suppression of the 1924 Soviet coup in Tallinn. The attempt to overthrow the government left the whole country feeling unsure and vulnerable for years. Many strands in Estonian-Russian relations went directly or indirectly back to December 1924, the events that had shaken the country.

The coup had been badly planned and was therefore not difficult to put down, but there was blood. An Estonian government minister was among the dead. The surviving communists were either arrested or shot and this curbed the feared spread of communism. Estonian historian Hannes Walter concluded that this fully justified the 25 Estonian dead. "Without a failed uprising it would have never been possible in the democratic Estonian Republic to shoot nearly 200 communists in a few days and actually physically eliminate the Communist Party and the danger of communism altogether. Thus, the uprising that had to end in a failure was in the interest of Estonia in every way and justified the moderate number of victims."[9]

Ernest Boyce, another of Brian's predecessors, said of the coup that the "tiresome Estonian Bolsheviks in Russia" had been encouraged by Moscow to go back home and cause mayhem.[10] Estonia had signed a border treaty with Russia in 1920, but the border remained porous. Estonia's answer was to declare all border areas, railways and the capital Tallinn to be under one or another form of emergency practically all through the eleven years that Brian spent in the country.

Moscow meanwhile kept a watchful eye on the Estonians who had crossed the border into the Soviet Union: they were often perceived to have done so with ill intent. This was called "speculation" – selling goods for profit – or simply contraband which in a number of cases involved cocaine, but was often interpreted as spying. At one point Russia freely admitted that it had shot 20 Estonian spies.[11] Spying was rife, or at least accusations of spying, as both Estonia and Russia needed information about their neighbour while eyeing each other with mistrust. In the 1920s and the early 1930s spy exchanges between the two countries were frequent.

Big spy trials were held. One of them, in St Petersburg in 1926, implicated Britain and left one of Brian's predecessors, Ronald Meiklejohn, agitated. The Soviets were aware that Estonia was collecting information for the British on Russian soil and that the British were benefiting from the spy network the Estonians had built in the country. Forty-eight persons had been charged with espionage on behalf of Estonia. Although there was talk of evidence of British involvement, nothing damaging was produced in court. A London newspaper reported: "Allegations were also made concerning a British intelligence officer and a former Russian colonel, who are stated to have been in charge of preparations for attacks along the Russian-Esthonian frontier line and for blowing up of Russian property including the Leningrad waterworks and the Gatchina aerodrome and hangars. Large sums of money are said to have been put aside for this purpose."[12] Colonel Frank, described as a British spy in Narva, an important border town, was named as the spymaster.[13] Of the 48, one was acquitted, 13 were sentenced to death by shooting, four were given ten years in prison and the rest got prison sentences of varying lengths.

A big communist trial was held in Tallinn in 1932. The communists were Estonians who had come from Russia and were arrested in Tallinn. Some sympathisers were also arrested, two printing presses, typewriters and an archive were seized. A total of 38 communists were tried and some of the court exchanges were heated. The court heard that money "from abroad" had motivated quite a few of the defendants (defence argued that doing something for money was no proof of communist beliefs), confessions were allegedly obtained under duress (Estonian security police had been to London for training, it was said), some defendants admitted party membership with pride, some denied any links with communism. Five were sentenced to 12 years of forced labour, eight persons, two of them women, got ten years of forced labour, four persons were given six years of forced labour and three were acquitted. Once again the Estonian police felt the communist party's activities were paralysed. It was estimated that of the 200 communists in the country only 20-30 remained at liberty.[14]

Moscow had its own spies on the ground, often working at the Soviet embassy in Tallinn. The Estonian Foreign Ministry's information department produced regular reports on Soviet embassy staff. Several were caught and expelled. One of them was Sergei Pavlovich Borisov, who arrived in Tallinn in the summer of 1934, having already done some spying in Finland in his previous post. In Tallinn where he was secretary in the consular section he inherited a network of agents; one of them was Nikolai Nei, an Estonian. Arrested by the Estonian political police, Nei promptly confessed. He had been working at Narva police station and the location enabled him to provide Borisov with lists of foreigners who crossed the border – something that Borisov had requested. There was particular interest in British citizens, also in British contacts with Russian emigre organisations in Estonia. Borisov was subsequently declared a *persona non grata* and left Estonia in December 1935.[15] This left thirteen Soviet agents in Estonia, but no "resident". Moscow saw a need for further recruitment. Brian's activities were reported by L29, L42 and L45.[16]

Brian has left no records about his own agents, but his colleague Leslie Nicholson has explained how he created a network in Riga: "It was a long and often heartbreaking job to find the right types and put them to work. As in most professions, espionage involves a great deal of planning and much careful preparation. The glamour attributed to it chiefly exists in works of fiction. Contrary to popular belief, agents are not usually met in cafes, bars or night clubs but are in most cases contacted in private flats. They are not even contacted direct, but sometimes through as many as three cut-outs so that nobody knows anything about anyone else." Nicholson also included words of warning, since he was aware "of dozens of unscrupulous agents of all nationalities who would sell their services to the highest bidder – with little compunction, at a later date, in passing the same information to the opposition, though at an increased price." He found that much information in Riga had been "planted by rival German and Russian agents for their own purposes."[17]

If Nicholson used cut-outs, it is logical to assume that so did Brian, but information often slipped through. There were so many opportunists and hangers-on around, eager to earn a bit of money for small services. Take the case of Andrei Salza, for example. He had worked for the British and named Capt Alec Ross, Brian's predecessor, and a man called Pantelejev as his handlers. He was no longer working for the British when he was interrogated by the Estonian political police, and yet he knew to name Brian Giffey. The information that he had passed on to the British had come from his work for the Estonian counter-intelligence in Narva.[18] The town, close to the border with Russia, was an important garrison as well as transit town. Salza was a distant relative of Adm Hermann von Salza whom the Estonian government had trusted to send to Geneva in 1932 as adviser at the disarmament conference. The admiral was said to be very pro-British and speak good English, so it is possible that Andrei may have indeed worked for the British.[19]

Andrei Salza, however, teamed up with another man from Narva, Aleksei Haritonov, who was a petty thief and a thoroughly dubious character. Together they hatched up a plot that was to provide Haritonov with cash and Salza with a fresh opportunity to work for the British. Haritonov, living in the border area, was in the habit of crossing illegally into Russia. Salza gave him a handful of British names that the young man was to take to Leningrad and trade to the Soviet authorities for cash. The plan, however, backfired when Haritonov changed his mind, went to Tallinn instead, intent on spilling the beans at the Soviet consulate there, but was recognised as wanted in connection with an unrelated crime and handed over to the Estonian police. Interrogated now by the Estonian political police, Haritonov readily told his sorry story and named the names. He knew the Estonian spymasters Roman and Nina Frank in Narva. (One of the Franks had been named at the Leningrad trial in 1926; Nina Frank worked at the Estonian army headquarters in Narva before emigrating to California.) Haritonov also named the following "British agents": Col Boris Sevastjanov, Nicolai Weymarn, Arseni Zhitkov, Col Wasilkowski, Coupje de Colong and Brian Giffey – all in Tallinn; Leo Hoffmann in St Petersburg, Rafael Farina in Riga and Pantelejev in Berlin.[20] The Estonians eventually found him guilty of gathering secret information for the Soviets (he had obtained a map of the explosives store in Narva for a friend who intended to sell it to the Russians) and gave him a 7-months prison sentence.

Why Salza trusted an opportunist like Haritonov with sensitive information (and promises of more about an important British spy about to arrive in Estonia) remains a mystery, but some of Haritonov's names were surprisingly up-to-date, since Brian Giffey had only recently arrived in Tallinn and Rafael Farina had only recently departed from Riga.[21]

Fate, however, dealt harshly with Haritonov. Having served his prison term in the Republic of Estonia, the young man, aged 31, was arrested again when the Soviets overran the country in 1940. The new masters labelled him an Estonian spy and found him guilty of spying against the Soviet Union. He was sentenced to death and was probably shot.[22]

Brian need not have faced men like Haritonov, but there must have been some of his kind among his sub-agents. Plenty of small crooks like Haritonov eked out an existence in Estonia, many of them stateless persons. In 1933, for example, Estonia unmasked 59 Soviet spies (of whom a few were serving soldiers) and a number were swiftly locked up for years. The border area running south from Narva was populated by poor and uneducated farmers who asked no questions when somebody, even a Soviet officer, came along and offered money for carrying messages or parcels. Rudolf Stilling was one of those imprisoned for eight years for acting as a courier for the Soviets. By the time he was released in 1935, aged 69, he had lost all his teeth and was in poor health. Estonia showed no mercy. Although he had served his sentence, he was banned from returning to his home farm near the border because he was still a security risk. He pleaded with the authorities, intent on joining his four sisters on the farm, but his appeals were rejected and he was forced to live by himself at Petseri some distance away. He died before the 1939 amnesty that lifted the domicile restrictions.[23]

Soviet intelligence files provide a considerable amount of information about Brian Giffey's agents, who may well have relied on characters like Stilling at one time or another. Numerous military men were among Brian's agents. Jeffery's MI6 history confirms what was known to the KGB some 70 years ago: the British passport control officers enjoyed a direct link to the host country's chief of staff and the head of the General Staff's 2nd department; they were known to the country's police and intelligence services and in many cases collaborated with them.[24] Among Brian's agents were, for example, Col Arnold Sinka (43941), Arnold Nõmm (43945), head of the Russian section at the General Staff, a nameless former head of the operations section of the General Staff (43996), a former military attaché in Moscow (43941) and a former head of the Russian section of the General Staff (43915). Johannes Santpank (43281) commanded the Estonian Navy from the autumn of 1939 and provided regular information on Soviet vessels entering Estonian waters. Olaf Kuldvere (43317) drafted shipping legislation at the Waterways Department.[25]

There was also a physician, Emil Laur (43514), on Brian's books.

The details come from the Soviet files on British intelligence that were initially set up in Moscow in the 1920s. Every little scrap of information was preserved and filed away for future use. The Soviets were diligent in gathering all kinds of details down to social gatherings and descriptions and habits of individuals who might be of interest. No British activity in Tallinn was above suspicion. Meanwhile Estonia, a small and young country, welcomed the friendly advice and assistance offered by London.

Claude Emery originally arrived to instruct Estonian pilots, but stayed on to do business. Peter Leslie was the temporary consul in Tallinn before Britain even recognised Estonia; he returned as acting consul in 1930 and stayed for several years. Alec Ross was initially adviser at the Estonian Finance Ministry and only then became a passport control officer. British-Estonian cooperation worked well ever since 1918 when the British navy saved the situation in the Baltic during the Estonian War of Independence. Help, as it turned out, was deemed to have been mutual and two Estonians, Gen Laidoner and Admiral Johan Pitka, received the honour of a KCMG for their assistance to the British. Moscow, however, saw things differently: Pitka's son Andrei was close to Georg Malkov-Panin, who was one of Brian's agents. All Brian's associates were suspect.

With its finger on the pulse, Moscow was well informed about the succession of British passport control officers in Tallinn. The names were not always correct (and there is the matter of transliteration), but they knew that Ronald Meiklejohn, Ernest Boyce, Alec Ross, Sidney Steers and Brian Giffey were the men involved in intelligence gathering. Alexander "Sandy" McKibbin, a freelancer, was in their opinion "worthy of special attention". Consul Peter Leslie, a friend of Graham Greene, was described as a zealous Catholic; he, Steers and Major Ross were known to speak Russian. Ross had a Russian wife, but was described as a lightweight who liked his drink while Brian Giffey, an "honest pen-pusher", was said to be "the head of the passport section and key representative of the English intelligence police". Brian's language studies were known but no mention was made of his drinking habits. This alone casts doubt on Soviet intelligence gathering because Brian was a heavy drinker. Also, Moscow knew that Brian had a pretty wife, but Claire could not be described as such. She had stayed behind in London when Brian was appointed to Tallinn and, although she did visit, the "pretty wife", more likely than not, was a casual escort. Brian was not short of female company. Moscow also mistakely thought that the local English-language newspaper *The Baltic Times* was funded by the British secret service.[26]

There was a lot of passing traffic in Tallinn. Moscow's eye fell on Mary Magdalena Webb, a Russian married to an Englishman, who kept coming and going, sometimes travelling from Germany. She was of particular interest because at one point she was perceived to be "under some kind of special protection of Major Giffey who had especially arranged for the local police not to disturb her." Brian, however, suspected Webb of links with Bolsheviks and asked the Estonian police chief to make enquiries. She was said to have connections with the Soviet entrapment agency "Trest" that had been active in the 1920s. Among other things, "Trest" was blamed for the death of Sidney Reilly.[27] Many aspects in British-Soviet relations went back to "Trest". Moscow meanwhile was confident that Webb was spying for both Britain and Germany. She needed the cash, Moscow concluded.[28]

Arseni Zhitkov, a former Tsarist naval officer, was also of interest to both London and Moscow. He had been hired by Boyce who invited numerous Russian émigrés to work for him. Zhitkov similarly had links with "Trest" and knew Roman Birk, the Estonian military attaché in Moscow who turned out to be working for the Soviets.[29] All the same, Zhitkov provided useful information to the British although the KGB knew that he had also invented things. The file on British intelligence records lovingly, in several versions, the story Zhitkov had related about two Estonian agents by the name of Leesik and Kotkas, who successfully sold to the Soviets a list of British agents in the Soviet Union. The agents were duly arrested and shot. Afterwards it emerged that this had been a British ploy to eliminate KGB agents and the Soviets had fallen for it. Moscow complained to the Estonian government, Leesik and Kotkas were taken to court, but were acquitted.[30]

In 1933 the KGB put Zhitkov's involvement with the British firmly in the past: his disassociation was seen as having ended a poor period of British intelligence gathering in Tallinn. Meiklejohn, a collector of rare birds' eggs, was recalled, since inadequate or outright false information had been sent up to London, and young Major Ross was brought in to clean up the act. "Ross's actions brought along a gradual but final exclusion of Zhitkov, the recall of Boyce and a big cut in the lines of work, collaborators and so on, which meant that there was a considerable overall reduction in the credits from the centre." Ross tried his best for three years "but his own attempts to arrange and lead the intelligence apparatus brought no success," the KGB concluded. He did not even manage to get the full cooperation of the Estonian intelligence bodies.[31] At this point Brian Giffey arrived on the scene.

British failures were observed also by an American in Riga. Maj W. Shipp, the US military attaché, sent regular reports to Washington in the early 1930s. He heard from a "very reliable" source that "the British Passport Control Officers have paid high prices for forged documents relating to the Red Armed Forces," and that much of the information had been just copied from a general book on chemistry.[32] As to individuals, Shipp quickly labelled Brian and his counterpart in Helsinki, Harry Carr, "British spies against Russia". Shipp had no doubt that both were either serving or former army officers.[33] The British military attaché in the Baltic states, Major Cox, had no responsibility for Russia, Shipp said. Cox did not even read the Red Army press because Russia was under the tender care of Giffey and Carr.

Of his relations with the British, Shipp said laconically, if peevishly: "This office has in recent years avoided any relations with the British Passport Control Service as it was found that the relations with this service were not satisfactory."[34] By the looks of it Shipp did not warm to either Brian or Carr. He was altogether deprecating about British intelligence gathering because, in his opinion, the officers used "an uncoordinated system of obtaining information about the Red Armed Forces which probably leads to considerable duplication and inaccuracy." He also noted that "the British Passport Control Officer in Riga (Harold Gibson) amounts to nothing."[35] Gibson was Leslie Nicholson's predecessor.

The KGB sounded positive about Brian Giffey's methods: "He, without fantasizing, based his work on links with the 2nd department of the General Staff and the political police." The Soviets wrongly identified him as a cavalry man and, surprisingly, described him as "rather rough". As to information gathering, Brian was said to be satisfied with what he obtained from the Estonians. Their military intelligence and police also benefited from the cooperation that smartened up their procedures. Furthermore, Brian paid for some information. The KGB, however, noted that the British were happy to take whatever the Estonians gave them while refraining from sharing their own information. Increasingly funding became a problem for Brian, as political relations between Britain and the Soviet Union improved.[36] There was less money for Tallinn when Britain started sending service attachés to Moscow from 1934.

It is almost amusing that an Estonian, "a certain Captain A.I. Kuk", had come very close to becoming the first Soviet service attaché in London four years previously. Having arrived unannounced at the British embassy in Moscow, he claimed to have been appointed a military attaché and requested a diplomatic visa. One was granted immediately. A swift but firm telegramme from London told the consul to cancel it: "We have never been consulted as is customary in these matters... We definitely do not want either to receive or appoint a Military Attaché in this instance. The Acting Consul General has made a regrettable and reprehensible error." The visa was duly cancelled and the Soviets posted Aleksander Kukk to Japan instead.[37]

In 1934, however, once the Americans had sent their service attachés to Moscow, London decided that "the advantages to be gained by the presence of a British Military Attaché in Moscow would more than offset the disadvantages of the presence of a Soviet Military Attaché in London. The Secretary to the Army Council proposed that the time had come for these mutual appointments to take place." The Foreign Office agreed.[38] Eric Skaife was appointed the British military attaché in Moscow and Alfred Collier, the air attaché. Collier had incidentally been the air adviser to the Estonian army in 1928-30. Vitovt Putna, a Lithuanian, became the first Soviet military attaché in London. The naval attaché appointments shortly followed. London sent Capt Henry Clanchy to Moscow in 1936 when Lev Antsipo-Chikunsky arrived in London as the Soviet naval representative. Both Putna and Antsipo-Chikunsky, however, suffered a terrible fate when they were recalled and executed in the 1937-38 Stalinist purges.

21. Officers of the 2nd department of the Estonian General Staff with their chief, Col Richard Maasing (seated, centre), 1935.

In many ways the KGB's information was remarkably accurate. Take, for example, the file on Col Richard Maasing, head of the Estonian military intelligence (2nd department at the General Staff). It demonstrates that the KGB knew more than 70 years ago that Maasing was a British agent whose code number was 43931 – something that was impossible to verify until Keith Jeffery's official history of MI6 confirmed it in 2011.[39] The numbering system itself was explained by Kim Philby (and published by Nigel West). Each country was assigned a number by MI6 (pre-war Estonia was 43), the head of station had three noughts after the country number (e.g. 43000) and he either inherited numbered agents or recruited new ones yet to be allocated numbers.[40] Brian Giffey was 43000 in Tallinn for eleven years. During this time he got to know Maasing well, visited his Tallinn office and often stayed "for hours".

Most of Brian's agents were Estonians. Quite a few were diplomats who had a military background or useful Russian connections, or both. Aleksander Warma was the consul-general in Leningrad, an observant and knowledgeable man when it came to military matters. August Rei (43447), a shrewd lawyer by training, was the country's ambassador to Moscow in the crucial years of 1938-40. August Torma (43470), who also had a legal background, had worked for the British during the Russian civil war and took a special interest in the Soviet Union when he was head of the Foreign Ministry's political department. He went on to represent Estonia in London 1934-71. Heinrich Laretei (43450), also a lawyer and military man, was ambassador in Moscow and in Stockholm 1936-40. Aksel Linkhorst (43452) was an attaché in Stockholm 1938-40.[41] Rudolf Möllerson (43910/A) was the ambassador and Ludvig Jakobsen (43442), the military attaché in Berlin. Only one foreigner, a Pole, Aleksandr Stulginski (43466) of the Warsaw

Institute, features on the KGB list, but Brian had other Polish contacts also.[42] The Poles were similarly gathering information on Russia and, at British suggestion, focused on sea transport between Germany and the Soviet Union.[43] Klaus Rosen, who had spent three years in London on an SIS training course, helped Brian keep an eye on the local Germans. And Arseni Zhitkov, having been written off in the late 1920s, resurfaced in the early 1930s and the Soviets saw him again providing information to both the Estonians and the British. In June 1940 the KGB made an attempt to turn him but without success.[44]

Maasing's deputy in military intelligence, Johan Tõnurist, was probably 43932, according to the KGB. (Unless it was Olav Mullas who had been in that job earlier, the KGB logic went.) Tõnurist was another good friend of Brian. Being a specialist in Soviet affairs, he encouraged Brian to recruit 43711 (Karl Kaplus, chief engineer on an Estonian steamship that often visited Leningrad) and 43711/a, who provided relevant shipping information. Similarly Col Evald Ein (43311), an Estonian Territorial Army (*Kaitseliit*) instructor on the island of Saaremaa, provided intelligence on the Soviet navy.[45]

The *Kaitseliit* was a well-run paramilitary organisation that acquired a new lease of life after the 1924 coup attempt. Brian was pleased to forge links with its highly motivated officers. Lt Evald Tart (43300), fifteen years his junior, helped him with agent recruitment and probably devised much of his network. Anni Giffey, Brian's second wife, knew Tart well, referred to him as "a very dear friend" and even said that "Brian loved him very much".

Brian seems to have had just two assistants most of the time (although the KGB mentioned six staff in 1936), one of them being Sidney Steers, officially the vice-consul, the other was probably Mike Turner. Nicholson in Riga (31000) gained

22. Kaitseliit men pose for a photograph.

the help of the Kentons in 1938 when they were transferred from Vienna. Kenneth Benton became Nicholson's assistant and his wife Peggie was the cipher clerk. It is thanks to Peggie Benton that we gain a glimpse into London's requirements on the Soviet Union. "Sometimes a request would come from Head Office to pay particular attention to reports on a certain factory, or signs that supplies of such and such a product were breaking down. Some of the most interesting articles were the obligatory pieces of self-criticism, when the manager of a big industrial combine or a state production unit would be selected to confess that output had fallen by x number of tons; that so and so many workers had been sent for corrective detention in Siberia; that the whole production of tractors from a certain works had proved unfit for use."[46] According to Nicholson, London's list of requests also specified the price it was willing to pay for any piece of information.

Having sent off the required information, Nicholson was often puzzled and frustrated by London's feedback, which seemed inconsistent to him. "Often a report compiled from accurate information slowly and painfully acquired, of which we felt rather proud, would receive scant recognition – probably, we guessed, because they had already obtained the information elsewhere. Other reports which we ourselves had rated lower might be more generously rewarded... Later on, in 1940, a short typewritten paragraph which gave the combined weekly output of German shipyards, fetched an immediate reward of £50."[47]

Nicholson's memoirs are entertaining; he was an excellent storyteller. One of his amusing stories was about the struggle to set up a wireless transmitter. It was eventually installed in a seaside dacha just outside Riga and Nicholson's love of boating was an ideal excuse for his frequent visits to the coast whenever he needed to communicate with London. Brian, too, loved boating, but there is no evidence of a transmitter in Tallinn. Instead there is evidence of British-Estonian cooperation in signals intelligence. A receiver, a radiogoniometer and other equipment were in 1932 sent to Estonia, with the aim of intercepting Russian cipher communications that were relayed to the Government Code and Cipher School in England for analysis. (The KGB meanwhile had an agent in Tallinn post office who intercepted a string of diplomatic telegrams.)

The 2nd department of the General Staff rented a house at Merivälja, a desirable coastal suburb of Tallinn, where staff were intercepting cipher telegrams in four shifts.[48] Flight Lt W.G. Swanborough of the Air Ministry's wireless telegraphy section visited Estonia in 1933. The archive files have retained much detail of the cooperation, including numerous quaint queries (translation, transliteration), but on the final count the experiment apparently had little intelligence value. The intercepts, however, continued to arrive in Britain until Estonia was occupied by the Soviets in 1940.[49]

The KGB was aware of two radio operators – 43350 and 43351 – and thought the latter might be Ervin Saar who had been a radio operator on Estonian ships and, later on, on passenger planes flying from Tallinn to Stockholm and Kaliningrad.[50] In the autumn of 1940 when Brian left Estonia, at least two of his agents were working in Helsinki: they were 43250, a radio operator handling Soviet wireless intercepts and Aksel Kristian (43933), former military attaché in Finland.[51]

Col Maasing, an upright and intelligent Estonian, found it impossible to remain in his country once it had painted itself into a corner by signing a mutual assistance pact with the Soviets in September 1939. He fled shortly after, initially to Germany. Subsequently he had a meeting with Brian in Helsinki, the Estonian police chief told the KGB two years later. "Giffey told me that, aware of Maasing's arrival time in Helsinki, he turned up at Helsinki station with the aim of establishing whether Maasing was being followed. In keeping with a pre-arranged telephone ring, Giffey and Maasing met in a Helsinki hotel room two or three days later... I learnt from Giffey that Col Maasing had been officially engaged by the German intelligence service. He had been specifically tasked to tour the Balkans, Hungary, Sweden, Norway and Finland. Giffey took advantage of his arrival in Finland to meet up. I also learnt from Giffey that soon after defecting to the Germans Maasing transferred his family from Berlin to Stockholm 'for safety reasons'."[52]

The police chief who provided this information, while betraying hardly any secrets that might harm Maasing or Brian, was Johan Sooman (43920), another Estonian with whom

23. *Estonian police chief Johan Sooman with a young assistant.*

Brian had a special relationship. Sooman was a respected officer and the KGB knew that the British had made him "a special payment for setting up an intelligence organisation on the Soviet frontier." He was considered "a valuable agent."[53] The KGB also knew that Sooman had a jealous rival, Tenson, who coveted Sooman's job that had been lost to him when the Estonian government fell in 1935. This made Tenson a potential target for recruitment. He had told a friend in the police about his grievances and about him feeling demoralised. Unbeknown to him, the friend was a Soviet agent (L47 by the name of Mölder) whom the KGB expected next to work on Tenson and, at a suitable moment, to recruit him. Tenson had once, in 1918-19, been bullied into working for the Soviets, so a second recruitment should not be difficult. Moscow thought that he would make another valuable agent.[54]

Anni Giffey has described how she saw Sooman approaching the British legation in Tallinn in the summer of 1940 when Estonia was under Soviet occupation. "Suddenly a car drew up opposite the Legation and then another car behind it... From the second car two men got out and went to the first car from which one of our friends – the chief of police – got out. He saw me and slightly nodded. He was arrested there and then. Did he want to come to the Legation for safety?"

Sooman, however, was soon released and Anni saw him again. She has related the encounter in central Tallinn as if writing to Brian. "You and I were walking on Narva Maantee, on our way home, when we met our friend the Chief of Police, walking with two men towards us. We were so pleased to see him free again and we all stopped. He drew you aside and said he cannot talk freely now but would you not meet him later, in the evening in the park where you could be undisturbed and talk. When you joined me and told me of this proposed meeting in this very secluded part of the park, very near to some buildings the Soviet Secret Police had taken over, I asked you not to go; if you wanted to go to take me with you and somebody else from the Legation. But Peter Gallienne [British chargé d'affaires] forbade you to go. I was relieved." Sooman was later sent to Russia and died there imprisoned.

The KGB also arrested Gen Johan Laidoner, the Estonian commander-in-chief, in 1940. More than a decade later he, a prematurely ageing man of 68, was interrogated in Russia and still remembered his conversations with Brian Giffey. Not revealing anything of Brian's work, he recalled his keen interest in improving his Russian skills and even remembered the book his wife Maria, a Russian of Polish extraction, had lent to Brian – *The Archive of Countess D*, a 19th century epistolary novel that Laidoner thought was well beyond Brian's linguistic abilities.[55]

In the tightly packed centre of Tallinn where streets are narrow and cobblestoned, Brian's office was located in a residential block at Vana-Posti 7-11 (house number 7, flat 11). His assistant Sidney Steers was in the same block, in flat 5. The premises had no diplomatic protection, much as MI6 in London had argued for diplomatic immunity for all its overseas staff.[56] From 1931 when Brian was at last promoted to major, he proudly displayed a bronze sign "Major C.K.O.B. Giffey" on his door. His regimental magazine called *Firm* congratulated him on promotion and noted that he had been selected to work "in outlandish parts", without specifying the country. [57]

24. *Vana-Posti 7 in central Tallinn where Brian and Sidney Steers had offices, 2014.*

The British mission in Tallinn was a short walk from Brian's office, at Lai 17 in the Old Town (today's Museum of Applied Art and Design). This is where the British minister for the Baltic states held office when in town; otherwise he resided in Riga. Joseph Addison was the minister when Brian first arrived. He was followed by Hughe Knatchbull-Hugessen, who was replaced by Edmund Monson and next Charles Orde took over. Wilfred "Peter" Gallienne came as the consul and chargé d'affaires in 1935 and even resided at Lai 17. His arrival brought a significant change because Brian soon found that he and Gallienne had much in common; they became friends.

Both had military backgrounds and Gallienne had been badly wounded in France in 1917, leaving him with a permanent disability.

Gallienne was concerned about Brian's security and therefore awarded him the title of second secretary. Not that it amounted to promotion. The Foreign Office treated it as a "local appointment" and omitted it from its records in London. Brian, however, was pleased to flash a card wherever he went, showing off his diplomatic title. He had another reason to be pleased with himself: contrary to the rumour the KGB had heard in 1933 about Brian's imminent recall, London was obviously satisfied with his performance and left him in post until the fateful events of 1940.

Chapter 6

Love is in the air

Anni and Brian's remarkable love story started in February 1934 when they were introduced by Laine Kallas. The latter was the gregarious daughter of Oskar Kallas, the Estonian minister in London, who made it her business to know everybody. She had played host to Anni Oras in London and was now, in Tallinn, helping the new English teacher, Ronald Seth, to find suitable accommodation. Mr and Mrs Seth had arrived all the way from Britain with a six-week-old baby.

Location for this first meeting was the fashionable Gloria restaurant in Tallinn. The orchestra struck up and Brian and Anni, having been introduced, duly danced. Brian was not immediately smitten: "She made no very deep impression on me as yet, but quite a number of impressions stuck – a very nice little girl, quiet and rather mouse-coloured, very modest and self-contained she seemed... Rather old-fashioned in fact... Yes, that was it: Victorian! Yet, with all her quiet simplicity, she had poise. And she was as slim as a fairy, and danced divinely, light as thistledown. "Further dancing opportunities followed and in May Brian thought that Anni was "a funny little kid, makes one feel one wants to be good to her. Rather like Alice in Wonderland – cross between a schoolgirl and such a wise little woman. Very colourless though – nothing to say for herself and no sex-appeal."

Brian was 47, a married womaniser and heavy drinker; Anni was 22, innocent and uncertain about her future. Her English was good because she had visited England at the age of 19 and subsequently spent a year there working as a home help. Her interest in England and the English language had been much encouraged by her elder brother, Ants, an established translator of English classics like Shakespeare, Shelley, Byron, Keats and T.S. Eliot. By the time Anni returned to Tallinn, however, she had not

25. *Johanna Elise Oras,* *better known as Anni.*

yet decided what to do with her life. All she knew was that she loved dancing. "It seemed to be my life and happiness – just to dance," she chirped.

It is unclear why she took no steps to become a professional dancer, but probably her father objected. Also, she tried to please a maternal aunt: "As I could not become a dancer, I thought I might as well become a hospital nurse," she said but, having merely begun, she quickly dropped the idea – "discipline was too awful." And so she was "the only child who was still at home, with no job, as father did not really approve of an office job, for which I was not trained anyway." She was often out in the evenings, with Laine Kallas keeping her company. "One party and dance after another and not a care in the world. Only father used to grumble about my never being at home, but as Laine was my chaperone, he let me go, as he had perfect confidence in her."

Anni's brother Ants Oras was the chairman of the Anglo-Estonian Cultural Society. The English language had suddenly become fashionable. Few had spoken it in the 1920s and Gen Laidoner, who in 1925 had negotiated the Estonian war debt in London, had had to use an interpreter when talking to the British authorities. In the 1930s, however, English began to be taught in schools and the English College was set up. Having just arrived from England to teach the language in Tallinn, Ronald Seth was roped in to deliver lectures to the society's 650 members, all very keen to learn. Brian gave a talk to describe the British constitutional system. However, the local colony was small and sometimes speakers were invited all the way from Britain. For example, Adm C.V. Usborne, former head of British naval intelligence, came over and delivered a lecture.[1]

Putting on English plays, and in English, may have been Brian's idea. He had produced shows before. In Persia, in 1918, his 9th Battalion had staged "a most comic show" and a ceremonial parade "under the orders of C.K.O.B. Giffey". In 1922, at the School of Military Administration, he had produced *French as He Is Spoke* and *Fancy Free* – "tremendous fun", he said.[2]

Brian's perceptions of Anni changed when she took to the stage. Nervous but happy, she must have been good because Brian saw her in a different light. During a performance of *Thark*, a farce by Ben Travers, he suddenly kissed her on the lips. "It came so unexpectedly that I almost forgot my lines and I was angry with you – so angry I wished I could hit you and hurt you. To you the kiss only meant just another kiss and to me it meant everything," Anni wrote later, as if addressing Brian. She had secretly longed for this moment, but when it came it had been witnessed by an audience and she was mortified. Rumours about Brian's womanising were rife and Anni feared that she might be seen as yet another conquest.

26. Dance band at the Estonia restaurant in Tallinn, 1931.

"I remember what a shock it was to me when I heard that you were married," Anni admitted, "and that your wife was coming out to you on a visit. You asked me to a big reception at the 'Estonia' – there were hundreds of people – your wife was there, standing by your side. She looked very much older than you, was charming in a rather mannish way, with a long cigarette holder and grey hair, and you so proud of her."

It soon emerged that Brian and Anni had genuinely fallen in love, a moment of declarations followed and by March 1935 they were discussing marriage. Brian was going to divorce his wife, Claire, and once he was free, he was going to marry Anni. "You told me a lot about Claire – her friendship and loyalty to you," Anni wrote. "How wonderful she was, so that I seemed to get to know her pretty well and accept her as part of you, as part of our future life together. Not so Nadja – your housekeeper – mistress. Of course the latter part had ceased, but she still lived in your flat, she was still your housekeeper. I got jealous, jealous of your past and everyone you had loved

– there were so many, apart from Claire and Nadja – Margaret and Billie and a score others – you told me about all of them, as we had agreed we'd not have ever any secrets from each other. How I wished then that I too would have had a 'past' so that I too could tell you about my past loves – all I had was Nicky – so absolutely innocent, and my friendships – but, alas – no lovers or affairs – I wanted to make you jealous so that you would know what it felt like – but I never could – I had no past." She had received three offers of marriage, which she had declined, and was still a virgin.

Happy times followed, alternating with anxiety. "I had told mother that I would stick to you even if there would be no divorce. Poor mother, she must have suffered a lot. She was deeply religious and to think that one of her daughters lived in 'sin' must have been very painful for her," Anni wrote at the time when divorce was not at all certain. "It was not all sunshine though – I was still jealous of Nadja, and she was still your housekeeper – we had misunderstandings – now and then I gave you back our engagement ring and told you to go to hell – I even smashed my favourite hand mirror father had given me years earlier – just to make you unhappy – you were a bit superstitious. It's been the same old story all my life – when I get angry I lose my temper and show it and it hurt you so – I myself forgot it as soon as I had had my outburst, but you have a long memory and were unhappy. But even so you wanted to marry me – my bad temper and all – we did love each other so."

There was concern about their age difference. "Mother may have been a bit worried that you were so much older than I," Anni said, "but Aunt Netty had consoled her by telling her that I needed someone older than myself – I needed a firm hand and an adult mind and you needed someone much younger than yourself – you needed to protect and spoil and look after someone young. She was right."

Brian was also worried. "Darling, don't you think you could love me as you have been doing for 6 – perhaps 8 years? Until I am 56?" he anxiously enquired. "Then I will live for four things only. First, to get divorced and for us to get married. Next, for us to have three happy, healthy children. All the time, to make you happy and to make money to leave you and our children. That I may not live too long. If you can love me some years, I shall not fear death but welcome it, for I must not live too long. I may be strong and fine and hold you till I am 56. God grant that I die before you love me less. Yours only, ever Ronny."

The sign-off shows how *Thark* continued to hold a special meaning for the couple. "Ronny" was the role Brian had played; it became a pet name and years later Anni's mother referred to him by that name. The drama group's most successful play, however, was *The Last of Mrs Cheyney* by Frederick Lonsdale. Brian both directed and played the lead. The play was so well received in Tallinn that it was transferred to Tartu, Estonia's second biggest city where Anni's brother Ants Oras was teaching at the university.

27. *Leading players of 'The Last of Mrs Cheyney' as drawn by Anatol Tofer. From left: Richard Kinghorn, Brian Giffey and Anni Oras.*

Anni had concerns about the divorce: "I had been worried about Claire, but you reassured me that it was not as I imagined – the real marriage had ceased already in 1916 and as well as you, Claire too had had her love affairs, and still had a permanent lover – that you were great friends and fond of each other, but that was all – she'd be sure to give a divorce, as she had always promised she would in case you were really in earnest."

A personal visit was required to start the divorce proceedings, so Brian and Anni travelled to London where they told a few (white?) lies. They declared that they were domiciled in England and gave a London address (Flat 18, Douglas Mansions, 120 Cromwell Road), boldly promising to be available for questioning if needed. Brian gave his occupation as civil servant, which was accurate in a way. It was also accurate to cite adultery as the reason for divorce, but the reader may find it surprising – the year was 1936. Even more surprising was the naming of Anni in the petition – she must have agreed to this. The court papers said that Anni and Brian were cohabiting at their London address and had "habitually committed adultery".[3] Divorce was also not cheap: £80 plus the surety of £50 – this amount would have paid a full year's rent for a small flat in central London.

Once back in Tallinn, the waiting game started. Divorce seemed not at all certain, particularly for Anni. "There were almost two summers and one and a half winters to get through and we had to wait and wait and wait. Will you get a divorce? These were anxious years, but years full of work and happiness, and fun too. Lots of parties, dances and badminton and skiing and bridge and our theatre in winter and bathing and yachting and tennis and long walks in summer, and as much as possible we were together and alone," Anni wrote with hindsight.

They continued to live at their separate addresses. Brian visited Anni in her home at Köleri 21-8 (and made several naked sketches of her), while his home was at Hollandi põik 4-9. Cohabiting was out of the question, discretion was essential. But they were able to go dancing and perform in plays (*Dear Brutus* by James Barrie, *The Roof* by John Galsworthy), spend summer holidays at Narva-Jõesuu or Loksa on the northern coast and enjoy yachting in the Bay of Tallinn in Brian's Kittiwake II. Whilst waiting, Anni continued to live much as before, without taking a job.

There were "kind friends" who, in confidence, told Anni about Brian's plans to leave for England and not marry her. "Town was full of gossip. Lots of people did not want to know me or recognise me any longer. I hated people in those days – but walked about with my head high. I did not want to give the people the satisfaction to see me dejected and afraid," Anni said defiantly.

Both Anni and Brian have drafted reminiscences about this period and much of this writing has survived. Of some incidents there are several versions, of some periods there is a complete silence. It is perhaps no surprise that Brian's job doesn't get a mention, although it was to determine much of their new life together.

Attitudes in Tallinn changed immediately once the decree absolute came through in October 1937. Anni appreciated the warmth coming from the British mission. "Peter and Rose Gallienne had always been very friendly to me, but of course they could not ask me to official parties to the Legation," Anni wrote, addressing Brian, as she often did. "But as soon as they knew that the divorce was a thing of the past and you were free again, they could not have been nicer and more helpful – I became almost overnight a member of the family of the British

Legation." Brian even found a positive angle to their long wait: "We would never have got to know each other so well, love each other so deeply and known who our true friends were if it hadn't been for this long wait of two and a half years."

28. Wedding of Anni Oras and Brian Giffey on 1 December 1937. From right: Hilja Oras, Brian, Anni, Dagmar "Dagi" Kiausch.

As if to compensate for the delay, Brian and Anni had not one, but three wedding ceremonies. The first one, on 30 November at the Estonian Register Office, was witnessed by a fellow Brit and amateur actor, Richard Kinghorn, and Anni's married sister Helmi Kiausch (better known as Totti). The second ceremony followed on the same day, led by Peter Gallienne at the British consulate. The third one came the following day, 1 December, at the Dome Cathedral, with Bishop Bernhard Rahamägi, the country's most senior cleric, officiating. Rose Gallienne remarked that the bride looked like a pretty little snowflake in the white velvet dress Brian had designed. Anni, happy and proud, was suddenly overwhelmed by her change of nationality: "I'm British now – a foreigner in my own country. With one simple signature I renounced my nationality, my country and became a foreigner."

Snow fell as the couple left Tallinn for their honeymoon. Some friends thought it was cruel of Brian to take his young bride on an eight-day voyage on the North Sea, but Anni was content, even when they arrived at Hull in a snowstorm. Everything went well in London where Anni had her first meeting with Claire, Brian's ex-wife. Anni found her "very, very charming". There was also a meeting with Nadja, who until recently had been Brian's housekeeper, but had since moved to England. The newlyweds visited the Estonian legation at 167 Queen's Gate where Oskar Kallas, whose daughter had introduced them in the first place, had been replaced by August Torma, who had occasionally acted as a courier for Brian. And there was Mrs Torma, another friendly face. "Alice [Torma] told me years later how sweet she found us – you so terribly proud of me and I looking up to you as to my God," Anni wrote in her reminiscences.

As Brian believed that he was Welsh, he took his bride to North Wales. "When we arrived at Llanrwst," Anni said, "it was dark and it was raining. We were both pretty tired and there wasn't a taxi anywhere. But Brian talked so nicely to the porter, as he always does – people are always happier after Brian has had conversation with them – and he got us a car at last – and we got to Trefriw – to paradise!" She was in raptures over the landscape; she loved the mountains visible from the hotel window. "We walked fast to get warm," she said of day two in her enthusiastic but not always grammatical English. "The further we went the more beautiful the scenery, till we arrived at a lake surrounded by mountains – it was so quiet there – no other sound but the burbling of a brook – not a soul anywhere. And I, Anni, see it all with my own eyes! – not read about it in a book, or see it in a film. It is real, true. I'm in the mountains, and with Ronny – but now I can always be with him – how happy I am."

Shy and fearful by nature, Anni was frightened by the cry of an owl and pleased to be held and comforted by her man. However, there was enough curiosity in her to want to see Brian's London haunts after the Christmas spent in Wales. They went to the Naval and Military Club on Piccadilly and to Brian's office where he proudly introduced her to his colleagues and superiors. In her notes Anni has disarmingly said that she needed Brian to "protect me, to guide my first faltering steps into the Big International World and Society." She was 25 years old.

By that time, however, Estonia had withdrawn from the big international world. President Konstantin Päts, who had seized power in March 1934, was ruling as a benign dictator. Nationalist ideas became dominant, crowding out the broader picture; political parties ceased to exist and critical thinking was dormant. The coup had been quiet, there was hardly a murmur of protest, even when it turned out that Päts tolerated no criticism. Foreign diplomats were compliant. A photograph dated January 1937 shows the diplomatic corps solemnly trooping out of the presidential palace at Kadriorg where the men, Peter Gallienne and Brian Giffey among them, had been wishing the president a happy new year.

Estonia was pre-war Europe's only happy country, American writer Marion Foster Washburn concluded. She had travelled all over the continent in order to write *A Search for a Happy Country*. The timing of her book, alas, was most unfortunate: it was published in 1940, the year Estonia lost its independence. It is curious that Ants Oras, Anni's brother, chose to promote the book in the post-war years. He must have seen it symbolising the devastating loss the nation had suffered. This allowed him to overlook the unhealthy dose of complacency and self-delusion of the 1930s Estonia that encouraged isolationism.

29. The diplomatic corps at Kadriorg Palace on 1 January 1937.
(From left): Peter Gallienne, Brian Giffey, Nuri Batu
(Turkish ambassador), Jean Helleu (French ambassador), Heuman
(head of office at the French embassy) and I. Gilberts
(first secretary at the Latvian embassy).

"Estonia has never wanted to be involved in world politics and has no wish to be so in the future. We will leave this to the Great Powers; they are responsible for European peace and security," said Julius Seljamaa, the foreign minister, in 1934, summing up Estonia's aspirations.[4] Gen Laidoner, whom Päts made commander-in-chief in the coup, was confident in January 1939 that there would be no war and, in August, when the news came that Germany and Russia had concluded a non-aggression pact, he still maintained that war was unlikely or, even if there was one, it would only affect Western Europe, not Estonia, and England would emerge victorious.[5]

Estonia decided on a neutrality policy. At the outbreak of war in 1939 the government instructed its minister, August Torma, to reiterate this policy at the Foreign Office in London. Meanwhile the consul Gallienne told the Estonian journalists in Tallinn that their country was "too neutral".[6] This neutrality was soon put to a test over a Polish submarine. On 15 September the Orzel entered the port of Tallinn, having developed a technical problem. The Estonians immediately interned her, confiscating her charts. And yet, on 17 September, once it was known that the Soviets had invaded Poland, the submarine managed to escape. Someone must have provided the necessary charts despite the Estonian watch over the ship. Who could that have been?

There are several versions, and one of them says that Brian Giffey went aboard to see the captain and, on hearing that he was ill, left a calling card with "God bless you" and "Good luck" scribbled on it. A rumour, however, soon started that Brian didn't leave a card, but delivered the charts needed for the escape. The technical fault, or even the captain's illness, was not discussed that much. Anni in her memoirs has suggested that the captain indeed needed Brian's help: "The submarine had got into Estonian Territorial Waters and was interned and the officers and crew were allowed out on parole. The captain came to see you, darling, for advice and help – I do not remember what part you played in it all – only remember that I sent the crew some flowers and some sweets and a little note with 'God bless you' or something like it – anyway, they escaped." Anni seemed pleased that the ship had slipped away. She was perhaps unaware that the escape brought about two Estonian officers' downfall. And there was more to come.

The Estonian authorities were confident that Brian effected the delivery of charts, according to a propaganda officer's memoirs. Brian sent either whisky or cognac to the crew, with charts hidden in the packaging. Another story, untrue it seems, accused the Orzel of sinking a Soviet ship, the Metallist, in the Baltic. The Orzel, however, proudly arrived in the British waters in October and brought London valuable information, probably about the mines in the Baltic.[7]

Moscow meanwhile had had its predatory eye on the Baltic states for some time. It reacted badly to the submarine's escape and used it as a pretext to bully Estonia into signing a mutual assistance pact in September. If the country could not properly intern a foreign ship it needed friendly help, the Soviet argument ran. The Estonians baulked at the idea of the Soviets setting up military bases in their country – the Soviets' key demand – but there was no alternative. President Päts had ruled out military resistance because this would lead to bloodshed. And so Estonia signed on 28 September and accepted that 25,000 Soviet troops would be put on its soil.

Gen Laidoner fell in with Soviet ideas and issued stringent rules that forbade photography of Soviet soldiers and cut off communications with the outside world. His instructions meant that

30. Gen Johan Laidoner.

Gallienne had to secure special permits for the British subjects who wanted to stay in Tallinn and other named locations where they might come into contact with the Soviet military. He reported to London that permission had been refused to ten or twelve people out of about a hundred.[8]

To highlight the relevance of these past events for today's world, the agreement between Ukraine and Russia that was breached in March 2014 by the annexation of Crimea allowed, by curious coincidence, the presence of as many as 25,000 Russian soldiers on the Crimean peninsula. The arrangement worked for over a dozen years before the events that led to the annexation. In Estonia the 1939 agreement worked for a shorter period, for nine months. In the course of those months problems arose and Russia cleverly separated out each of them as and when they arose. This took a lot of Estonian energy and allowed the country to take its eye off the ball.

31. Former British legation at Lai 17, Tallinn, 2014.

If the Orzel had not managed to escape the Soviets would have probably found some other pretext with which to intimidate Estonia. London meanwhile wanted to support its ally Poland and Brian played a small but significant role in the events of 1939. He had enjoyed excellent cooperation with the Poles in Tallinn, particularly as regard to shipping information. One of the Poles, Aleksandr Stulginski (or Stulczinski), was his agent (43466). Brian probably helped the Orzel to escape.

Anni Giffey was sworn in by Gallienne in September 1939; all hands were needed on deck. She became "a member of the Legation Staff – cypher clerk and general dogsbody", as she put it. It was a time of high uncertainty and many rumours. The legation in Riga heard that the staff in Helsinki had been evacuated and the passport control office in Tallinn had been closed, but there was no way of checking because the telephone line was dead.[9] Gallienne in Tallinn felt responsible for the 190 British subjects in the country, 26 of them children. Although assurances had been given, he did not feel confident about their safety. "I personally am not so sanguine, but it would be unwise to give voice to my fears in Estonia. Aggressive action by Soviet Russia seems to be contingency which should be considered," Gallienne told London.[10]

Gallienne soon ordered Anni to leave Tallinn for her own safety, with her husband's connivance, she suspected. So she worked at the legation in Helsinki for two weeks, but was then sent to Stockholm for a month, together with other Helsinki women. She found the idleness and separation from Brian difficult to bear. She was also bitterly disappointed not to have fallen pregnant, a fact she mentioned more than once. To wish for pregnancy at a time of high uncertainty and war is strange, but Anni was young and immature. Brian had wanted a child, even three children, and Anni wanted to please her husband.

One wonders how she would have coped if a baby had come along. Also, a mere five years on she told her diary: "Children rather bore me, animals never." She was always very fond of cats and dogs.

While Anni was in Stockholm, Brian in turn was transferred to Helsinki. He teamed up with his counterpart Harry Carr, who had been in post since 1928. The two men knew each other well. The situation in Finland was tense; there was a stand-off with Russia. If Estonia had succumbed to Soviet demands and was bound by the mutual assistance pact, then Finland, having been presented with a similar ultimatum, rejected Soviet demands. As a result, the Soviets attacked the country in November in the so-called Winter War.

Brian, missing his wife, had time for introspection. He wrote to her every day, but few of the letters have survived. In one of them he made a surprise confession: "People who knew me in the old days just can't understand what has happened. When it's really so simple, that God has given me the perfect woman, that I sought in 100 others and found at last, that loves me entirely and in all ways and makes me perfectly and entirely happy." In the light of Brian's past this may not sound entirely convincing, but Anni also sensed a change in her husband. "And you changed so – you, who had always had a roving eye for a pretty face or a slim or not so slim ankle – all of a sudden had no eyes for any other female but me."

The Giffeys must have agreed early on to number their letters. The times were uncertain and the post unreliable. Brian's letter to Anni quoted above is number 220. Like many lovers before them, they wrote in an effusive style. Their letters are repetitive and full of small detail – trivia that is unimportant or outright irritating to an outsider. The messages were after all meant for their eyes only (although Brian later said they might be published one day). Husband and wife badly needed mutual encouragement and affirmation. It is obvious to the reader that they missed each other. Brian, keeping up his Welshness, often signed off as "Bron", while Anni was "Bryn". These pet names stuck for years, with Anni occasionally referring to her husband as "Bron, the great rock". Brian seemed to relish his position of physical and moral strength. "Of course, I have had my worries too," he told Anni, "but I am 'Bron'. I must be and pray to God, may ever be your strong support." They also liked to call each other "captain" (Brian) and "mister" (Anni, first mate).

Meanwhile in Tallinn thousands of Baltic Germans were preparing to leave the country in answer to Hitler's call to return to the Reich. Gallienne told London in October that the threat of "complete Bolshevisation of Estonia" underpinned the exodus. A shrewd observer, he saw the situation clearly: "The departure of the Balts and the entry of Soviet troops may be two different subjects, but from the point of view of Estonia they are closely connected. If Soviet troops had not been allowed to enter Estonia, and if Nazi circles had not spread the report that eventually there would be a reign of terror here, few Balts would have left."[11] Gallienne estimated that 16,000 Balts (Baltic Germans) would leave. This kept Estonian ports very busy. The director of Passport Control in London issued a warning to alert staff to potential Russian and German spies.

It is regrettable that Gallienne never wrote the book about Estonia he intended. He was a sharp-eyed watcher whose heart was in the right place. The way he described the 22nd anniversary of the Soviet 1917 revolution celebrated in Tallinn, "with ostentatious grandeur", goes a long way towards explaining the Soviet cunning. He said that dinners for 50 people were unusual in the city, but the Soviet legation had invited 150 to its banquet. "Every important member of the Estonian Government was present and all the diplomatic corps. The United States Minister refused to attend and did not allow any member of his staff to accept... M. Selter, the former Estonian Foreign Minister who had negotiated the Estonian-Soviet Mutual Assistance Pact, had first declined the invitation, but, I am credibly informed, received two pressing visits from Soviet officials which left him with no option but to accept."[12]

In Gallienne's opinion "Estonians feel that they are faced with extinction because of the rivalries of great Powers, and the defeat of Germany by the Allies would not save them." Meanwhile the Estonian army was being reinforced. "Munitions are being bought in Germany and Russia. Estonians believe that eventually they will fight, but against whom, and for whom, they do not know."[13] These were prophetic words because many Estonians did fight, if not directly for their homeland. Squeezed between two occupations (the German troops arrived in 1941), they fought either on the Soviet or German side, while insisting that their fighting was all for Estonia. They were not given any choice in the matter.

Meanwhile Soviet use of Estonian facilities in 1939-40 was seriously denting the argument about Estonia's neutrality. The Soviets found it convenient to bomb Finnish targets using Estonian airfields. Charles Orde, the British minister to the Baltic states, visited Tallinn in December and filed a melancholy report. He did not find the country in good form. "The average Estonian, I find, takes some malicious pleasure in the trouble which, as they think, the Finns have brought on themselves by being braver than the Estonians. No doubt it comes partly from a feeling that the Finnish predicament proves the wisdom of the Estonian surrender."[14]

The war brought a change to thinking in London once it became clear that Charles Orde was going to be transferred to Chile in the spring of 1940. London decided to demonstrate that each of the three Baltic states deserved a minister of its own. Gallienne, already established in Tallinn, was henceforth going to be the British minister to Estonia where the announcement was viewed as a sign of British support, something that Gallienne confirmed in an interview with *The Baltic Times*. "This step demonstrates decisively that the friendly interest which Great Britain has shown in the Estonian Republic since the day when she proclaimed her independence over 22 years ago, continues unabated," Gallienne said.[15]

The Foreign Office, however, maintained a cautious tone regarding its diplomats: "Their rank is to be purely personal and local and it is to be explained to them that their promotion is a war measure, that they will receive no extra pay or allowances, that their designation as Minister does not entail any permanent change in their status in the Service, and that on their transfer to another post they must expect to revert to their present seniority in the Consular Service."[16]

As President Päts planned to go on holiday, Gallienne plumped for the only available date – 7 June – for presenting his credentials. It was just ten days before the full Soviet occupation of the country. The Giffey household was also on heightened alert around this time: Anni had bad stomach pains that were diagnosed as appendicitis and her appendix was removed. "The surgeon, nice Mr Kirman, said it might have burst any moment and I would have been very, very ill indeed," Anni recalled. "I was given only a local anaesthetic and Mr Kirman asked me whether I would like to watch the operation – I did not."

32. Peter Gallienne's credentials ceremony at Kadriorg,
7 June 1940.
Seated (from left): minister Gallienne, President Konstantin Päts,
Foreign Minister Ants Piip. Standing: Col Herbert Grabbi (senior
presidential adjutant), Lt-Col C.S. Vale (British military attaché),
Elmar Tambek (head of presidential office), Artur Tuldava (protocol
chief), Peter Leslie (secretary at the British embassy), Brian Giffey
and Lt Jaakson (junior presidential adjutant).

Brian has filled in the missing context: "Thirteen days later the ruddy Russians occupied the country. A quarter of a million men of all arms poured into the country, a third or more of the Baltic Fleet entered the ports, and masses of Air Forces landed on all airfields – to overawe a population of only 1,150,000. The 17th June 1940." The timing was fiendishly clever since all of Europe was aghast at the fall of Paris. This is how the Republic of Estonia quietly ceased to exist.

Soon a Soviet-style puppet government took office in Tallinn, made up of Estonian communists who had, until then, been living in Russia. "Then came the comedy of elections," Anni wrote. "Elections were compulsory – one candidate only – a communist. And the result was, so the Russians declared: the whole nation, out of free will had voted to become a part of Soviet Russia. My people wanted to become part of Soviet Russia! If you would have seen the desperate longing for freedom – nobody wore red in those days. Everyone had a tiny flag with the national colours, everyone sang national songs – and they wanted to become part of Soviet Russia! The terrible, terrible irony, the tragedy of it all."

Gallienne marvelled at the stagecraft. "The technique employed by the Soviet Union in acquiring the Baltic States was masterly. Masterly, but ruthless and unscrupulous. As early as July 5th [when the elections were announced] it was obvious to foreign observers that Russia had at last decided that the moment had come to seize these States, but right up to the last moment – even in fact now – Estonians have refused to believe that this is their fate. Only last week directors of departments of the Foreign Ministry begged me for my opinion and it was obvious that they were hoping that I would say that I did not think Estonia would be made a Soviet Republic."[17] Gallienne knew that there had been many arrests and Gen Laidoner had been taken to Moscow.

Earlier Gallienne had been puzzled by the show trials of Moscow where the accused readily confessed, but now he began to see how they worked. "For the first time I understand the confessions of guilt in the many Moscow trials, for here I have seen Estonians publicly, and apparently voluntarily, confessing that their Government and their country have been guilty of a varied number of offences. The statements made by Ministers, the press, deputies and public speakers are generally untrue (with one exception) and ridiculous. The exception is that they accuse a number of members of the previous Government and their friends of being guilty of corruption – this is true. Many Estonians now deeply regret that last October Estonia did not refuse to permit the entry of Soviet troops and die fighting. If I write with some bitterness it is because I regard Estonians as a fine race, and feel that the method of their virtual extinction might have been less ignoble."[18]

Chapter 7

Flight from Tallinn

The situation in the summer of 1940 was tense. If in 1939, after the signing of the Estonian-Soviet mutual assistance pact in Moscow, Gallienne had not felt "much immediate danger of persecution of members of the British colony at Russian instigation", he now had second thoughts.[1] Anni knew of one reason for his concern: "The British Legation was not British property (the building), but only a rented house, and nobody really knew whether it was considered as 'British territory', so to speak – anyway, Peter Gallienne thought it advisable to get as many British subjects to come to the Legation, as nobody really knew what would happen – after all Russia and Germany had a neutrality pact at the time, and Germany was at war with Great Britain."

Rose Gallienne, the new minister's wife, had been sent out of harm's way to England, and that left Anni in charge of eating and sleeping arrangements. "The Russians had taken my beloved country Estonia," Anni later recalled, "and we at the British Legation did not know what would happen, would they try to force [their way] into the Legation?" There were some guns on the premises and willingness to fight if necessary. Gunshots were heard in the street late at night when Brian was out. Anni addressed him in her diary: "I was dreadfully worried about you, as I knew you were anything but popular with the Soviets, and their Legation [was] so very near. I could not rest, nor sleep."

"Then followed three months with the [ruling] Russians in the country, taking control of everything, arresting people, torturing them," Anni wrote. "There was no laughter, nothing cheerful. Life became a nightmare. People disappeared, friends committed suicide. When we met friends and acquaintances in the street, they turned away, and so did we; it was not safe for them to know us. At night Russian tanks came and came – and night after night one lay awake listening to the heavy roll of tanks and more tanks, or the Russian troops singing. One song only. Even now I seem to hear the tune and shudder."

Moscow ordered the British missions at Kaunas, Riga and Tallinn to close by 25 August. All foreigners were expected to leave by that time, but the date slipped. Anni and Brian left on 4 September. Brian recalled many years later, writing to his niece, Dagi: "If Anni and I had not been married when the blasted Russians took your country in 1940 I should have had to leave and she to stay. We should have been parted in despair, for years of dreadful anxiety, and the thought puts me in a sweat even now."

Anni found departure very hard. "The terrible, terrible knowledge that we had to leave my family behind. To leave them behind! To what fate, to what future? To be deported, imprisoned, shot? I was desperate, and could do nothing. I had to go and leave them... It is easier to be in danger oneself than to know your nearest and dearest to be, and not to be able to help." Having become a British subject, she had to leave, but she was very close to her mother and sisters. In her own style of English she said ruefully: "When our ship left for Finland and I was standing on deck and looked back at Tallinn – where

I was born and where I grew up, where I fell in love and was married. Where all I loved were, where my home had been, security, my very roots – Tallinn, so beautiful in the early morning mist. Tallinn which had been so happy and carefree – now a prisoner, a wounded, unhappy and hopeless town."

33. Kaitseliit men and women assemble for an exercise in the 1930s.

Brian's thoughts have not survived but he no doubt worried about the agents he was leaving behind. He had built close links with a number of men in town. Would they be safe under the Soviets? Also, the Giffeys had in Tallinn witnessed the funeral procession of a distinguished woman-officer of the Territorial Army (*Kaitseliit*) who had committed suicide. Brian said to Anni: "I hope we'll never be brought to envy her for having escaped what's coming to us." Brian knew a great many men and women in the *Kaitseliit*; he must have thought of Evald Tart in particular. Tart was an agent as well as a personal friend. He did well, however, when the Soviets first arrived: he was employed as a foreman on a construction site.

34. Evald Tart in 1940.

Ferdinand Schmiedehelm (43382), an Estonian naval officer, was one of those arrested by the KGB in 1941 and shot. Aleksandr Stulginski (43466) was also arrested but was subsequently freed under a Soviet-Polish agreement, since he was a Polish citizen.[2] By the autumn of 1941 Estonia was occupied by the Germans.

The arrival of the Germans was initially welcomed by many Estonians. They were seen as liberators. With time, however, it became clear that theirs was just another occupation. Ordinary citizens continued to disappear as before. The new masters found informants who helped them unravel Brian's connections and MI6 became concerned that some of its sources in Estonia and Russia might be compromised. One of the informants was said to have been Georg Malkov-Panin.[3]

The Giffeys knew Malkov-Panin well; they had enjoyed week-ends and cross-country skiing together. Malkov-Panin was a naturalised Estonian born in Finland, who partnered Sandy McKibbin in his timber business. McKibbin, born in Russia and therefore a Russian speaker, also enjoyed a Finnish connection through his wife. Sandy and Helmi McKibbin lived in Tallinn for nearly two decades. Brian said that McKibbin was "one of the grandest fellows in the world." However, McKibbin's timber business failed and this may have created tensions. Why else would Malkov-Panin share with Germans the information he had picked up from Brian and McKibbin? And he can't have known much.

On the other hand, a number of Estonians worked for the German Abwehr (German military intelligence) before the war while also working for the British. Links within the spying fraternity were complicated. Brian for example knew in 1939 that Col Richard Maasing was close to the Germans and would not have been able to flee from Estonia without their help. And McKibbin in Tallinn befriended the German spymaster Alexander Cellarius. After the 1940 Soviet takeover McKibbin left Estonia for Sweden where he became a full-time MI6 officer. Brian continued to think of him as "a most admirable man; rarely have I met such a combination of grand enthusiasm and sound common sense."[4]

Meanwhile Kim Philby joined MI6 in London. By the autumn of 1941 he had secured a position within the organisation that allowed him access to sensitive information. It is not known what information exactly he shared with the Soviets, but anything of no immediate value to Moscow was simply filed away. Nothing was discarded. A large number of files were opened on British agents. Philby identified Richard Maasing, for example, as a British spy in 1942.[5] At that time Estonia was German-occupied, so the file on him had to wait. Even after the war there was a wait until a local KGB branch was set up in Tallinn. Later still many files were transferred from Moscow. In some cases new files had been created in Tallinn and those were merged with the Moscow material. Tallinn also began to submit regular reports to Moscow and there was some general correspondence. In the 1950s a serious hunt was on for interwar British agents.

The KGB did not want to risk finding that there were still live British agents in Estonia, but even more pressing was the desire to turn the survivors. It was a slow process in the course of which relatives and friends had to be found and interrogated. Moscow had honed its technique over the years and used the existing personal details creatively. Anybody arrested could be bullied, using the information on file. In the absence of comparable British sources the archive in Tallinn is certainly valuable, even if information was obtained under duress. Estonia's own intelligence materials were unfortunately destroyed in 1939, and even this fact is known thanks to KGB files.[6]

In 1943 the KGB knew the code numbers of 55 of Brian's agents and 25 of Nicholson's in Riga, but very few of the numbers came with names.[7] Agent reports sent to London used only code numbers and Philby apparently had no access to agent names. By 1955, however, the KGB had identified 39 of Brian's agents, which left sixteen still unnamed. The KGB's task was complicated by the fact that tens of thousands of Estonians had fled their homeland in 1944 to escape a second Soviet occupation; they ended up as displaced persons and then as émigrés scattered around the globe. The Soviets kept sifting through the information its agents were collecting, slowly but steadily, in an effort to put names to numbers. It was a colossal undertaking.

It is interesting to follow the KGB logic, for example, in its attempts to identify 43288. There was scant detail: the man was Estonian and he had been the chief engineer aboard the Pearu. After some deliberation, two candidates remained: the man sought was either Franz Pull or Bernhard Egenfeld. Both had worked as senior mechanics on the steamship. Franz Pull had died in the war but his widow and son had survived, so the KGB's instinct was to tackle them for further information. Egenfeld was alive, working at a Tallinn meat-packing plant. The KGB decided to put pressure on him, too.[8]

In a similar vein, Juhan Lootsaar was suspected of having been 43324. The code had been allocated to an artillery officer, and Lootsaar seemed to fit the bill. Furthermore, Lootsaar knew Evald Tart who had advised Brian Giffey on agent recruitment – all pointing in the right direction. However, the Soviets remained cautious and drew up a plan involving several persons who were to be bullied to make sure that Lootsaar was their man. Lootsaar's relationship with Tart was also to be scrutinised.

Lootsaar was close to another British agent, Ludvig Jakobsen (43442), who had been turned by the KGB in 1940 (becoming agent "Stok") while living in Germany where he was the Estonian military attaché. He was also known to work for the Abwehr. "Reading these documents the inevitable impression is that the KGB took advantage of the man's greed when recruiting him," an Estonian analyst has concluded. In postwar years Jakobsen ended up as a diplomatic spokesman for the then defunct Republic of Estonia in West Germany, but the KGB was still hoping to use him for its own ends to thwart British and US intelligence services. Jakobsen was elderly, his health was failing, but the KGB talks with him, with the help of his sister-in-law, were progressing satisfactorily. Jakobsen promised to provide the information the Soviets wanted, but then died.[9]

Postwar KGB bullying was nothing new; the KGB had a history of bullying techniques. In 1933, for example, an Estonian, Arnold Tulver, received a letter from Russia, from his ex-wife, urging him to visit because their child was seriously ill. Tulver duly obtained the necessary travel documents, but got only as far as Leningrad where he was taken aside and invited to join a radio operators' course. He was told that there was nothing wrong with his child, his documents were seized and he was told that only on completion of the course would he be free to return to Estonia as a Soviet spy. Although warned not to reveal recruitment details to anybody, Tulver next walked into the Estonian consulate where he related his strange story. On the following morning Tulver received a further threat from the KGB: he would be shot if he told anybody what had happened.[10] No wonder the Estonian consulate didn't take Tulver's story at face value because the Russians were known to be clever and devious.

The KGB was also more ambitious after the war, undaunted by great distances. Lt-Col Arnold Sinka (43941) was after the war in Sweden but moved to Australia by the 1950s. He had been the deputy head of Estonian military intelligence and the KGB entertained the hope of persuading him to infiltrate SIS for them. Sinka had already been turned in 1940 (as agent "Pavel") and provided information about Estonian officers. At the time he was the military attaché in Moscow. In 1955 the KGB found some of his relatives still living in Estonia and made them write letters to establish contact with the colonel. The plan was to use an Estonian sports coach (another KGB recruit) to deliver the letters, as he was going to the Olympic Games in Melbourne.[11]

A second line of approach was developed just in case. Erik Põld was recruited and trained in Soviet Estonia for a visit to Sweden where he was expected to meet up with Erik Laid. Both had been involved in anti-German resistance in Tartu, so Laid was likely to trust Põld. Laid himself was linked to British, Finnish and Swedish intelligence services and – highly relevant – was close to Sinka.[12]

Another of Brian's agents, Aksel Kristian (43933), had once, in 1936, been turned when he was waylaid in Leningrad. At the time he was the Estonian military attaché in Finland, but he had previously worked at the 2nd department of the Estonian General Staff, and so was able to provide information to the Soviets about Finland and Germany. Ties with him had broken since, but the KGB had located his sister in Estonia and planned to restore contact by sending her to Germany where Kristian had settled after the war.[13]

Considerable efforts were made to turn Richard Maasing (43931). He had been given the codename "Venal" (*Prodazhnyi* in Russian) because he could be bought by anybody, so why not turn him to work for the Soviets. In 1946 the KGB looked at the numbers of Baltic émigrés in Sweden and concluded that Maasing might play a significant role in harnessing this potential to work against the Soviet Union. He was also suspected of running agents in Soviet Estonia. Two years later it was known that Maasing had recruited 160 Estonians who were going to be trained in the US as parachutists and saboteurs. Efforts were made to secure the names of these recuits. In Tallinn meanwhile surviving members of Maasing's immediate family were hunted. It was important to find the right person to lean on; he/she had to travel to Sweden, get close to Maasing and gain his trust. Maasing meanwhile was known to have said that all recent arrivals, including defectors, were Soviet plants. All the same, the KGB had no intention of giving up; plots were hatched to corner him. "The plan to recruit Richard Maasing is yet another example that demonstrates how agency recruitment was an absolute priority for the KGB," an Estonian analyst has concluded.[14]

Maasing's nephew Heinrich Toots, who had worked for the Germans in 1941 and given them names of communists, was convicted of spying for Britain in 1948. He was said to have carried out espionage tasks ordered by Maasing and was given fifteen years in a Soviet labour camp.[15]

Tallinn was enthusiastic and inventive in its pursuits, but some of its plotting was never implemented because of a veto by Moscow. "It is possible that Moscow may not have wanted to infiltrate the British intelligence services from the Baltic region out of fear that the network could compromise the work of the Cambridge Five," two French researchers concluded.[16]

The Tallinn office even took an interest in turning McKibbin, who by the end of the 1940s had been transferred to London, recruiting and training Baltic agents to be sent back to their homeland. They were to make contact with local resistance. However, unbeknown to the British, the KGB had already eliminated the so-called Forest Brothers and replaced them with its own agents, which meant that practically all the men dispatched from London were caught on arrival or soon after. Philby had by then moved on to become head of station in the United States, but he still had access to some information about the Baltic operations. It is known that in 1951, for example, he attended an intelligence meeting at which McKibbin's boss Harry Carr discussed cooperation with CIA.[17] Philby is likely to have passed on to the Soviets whatever details he heard.

The KGB plans to turn McKibbin seem ambitious and implausible. However, information was carefully collected about his relationships and pressure was put on the individuals concerned. Vladimir Kolzakov (agent "Karasjov"), whose father, a White Russian colonel, had worked for McKibbin's timber firm and was trusted by McKibbin, was going to be sent to England to work at the Soviet trade mission. While there, he was expected to meet up with McKibbin and aim to turn him.[18] The Soviets were good at collecting compromising material and may have found out something unsavoury about McKibbin.

There was even an alternative plan, involving McKibbin's sister, Yelizaveta Viktorova, in Kharkiv, Ukraine. The local KGB branch had been instructed to put pressure on her. In Tallinn a Niina Andrejeva was said to be a close friend, so the KGB was working on her, too.[19] The plans to turn McKibbin seem to have stalled, however, when it became clear that the Baltic operations had failed and McKibbin was made a scapegoat for the failure.

Back in 1940, however, Brian knew nothing of Philby's treachery. Having fled from Tallinn in September, Brian and Anni spent four months in Helsinki, working at the British legation. After the comforts and servants of Estonia they found the Finnish capital gloomy. "Finland was recovering from the war with the Russians, and it was a sad picture and a cold winter with little fuel and little food," Anni recalled. Just before Christmas Brian was recalled to London. As flights were few and far between, Anni suggested they embark on a train journey via Leningrad and Moscow.

It is curious that they risked this circuitous and arduous route. Only a few months previously Anni had worried about her husband when gunshots were heard in the streets of Tallinn because Brian was "anything but popular with the Soviets". Brian, on the other hand, cannot have forgotten the 1933 trial in Moscow of six British engineers falsely accused of espionage and wrecking. They had been working for Metropolitan-Vickers, but were accused of links with the British secret service. Once arrested, they were kept in solitary confinement for more than a month, bullied and interrogated for hours. Isolation and pressure cracked some of them and one even pleaded guilty in court. All six were eventually released (five were expelled), but their high-profile trial left a nasty taste in the mouth. There were plenty of other, more recent trials involving Soviet citizens, in which the charges included spying. Brian no doubt was very much aware of the dangers involved although he and his wife had diplomatic visas.

35. Paul Oras, Anni's cousin.

Anni's first impressions of Leningrad were negative. The railway station was badly lit and cold, the people seemed glum and grey, the hotel comfortable but dirty. They were not allowed to stay overnight and, as Anni turned the bathroom taps and there was no water, this suddenly seemed like a relief. On the other hand, the couple enjoyed the food on offer and visited the Hermitage. Whilst being driven through the streets, Anni recalled the city's glorious past but curiously spared no thought for her cousin Paul Oras, who had left Estonia for a career in Soviet intelligence. He had lived most of his life in Leningrad.

Paul shared the fate of many talented and loyal Soviet people: he was arrested in 1937, accused of wrecking and spying, but surprisingly not executed. In December 1940 when the Giffeys were in town, he was in Shpalernaya Street prison (local KGB headquarters) close to the couple's hotel and the Hermitage. It is interesting to contemplate that this was probably the closest the two in-laws ever came to meeting. Brian must have known of Paul's existence and followed his career while Paul may have been oblivious to this new British connection. Paul was already behind bars when the Giffeys' marriage took place. Paul had trained as a naval engineer and was subsequently appointed naval attaché to Sweden, Italy, Greece and the United States. In captivity he had the dubious honour of designing ships, as the Soviets belatedly realised that many brainy individuals had been murdered in the purges and there was still a war to be won. He died prematurely in Butyrka prison in Moscow in 1943.

Anni met Paul just once when she was in her teens and Paul was visiting Tallinn. She took a strong dislike to him straight away and mentioned him in her recollections idiosyncratically and only in passing. She was putting together a kind of family tree. "Paul, who became an admiral in the USSR Navy, but was, presumably, shot in the great purge in the 1930s. He had married a Georgian woman and they had a son. We met them once in the early 1920s. I was terrified of Paul – he too had red hair. No idea what happened to his wife and son."

This is all she said. It is strange that she should have taken exception to Paul's red hair. Her father was a redhead and, as a surprise coincidence, so was Brian. So there must have been other reasons for her dislike of Paul. She must have heard stories of Bolshevik brutality. Paul had also chosen to turn his back on Estonia, marry a Russian speaker and live in a Russian-speaking environment – another possible reason for her dislike.

The Giffeys were generally lucky in their 1940 journey through Russia. In Moscow they were met by Capt Clanchy, the naval attaché. Stafford Cripps, the ambassador, found time for a chat. Meanwhile about 70 British subjects were still in Tallinn, thoroughly confused about the delay in their departure. One minute they were told to go to the station and board a train, the next minute they were told to get off again. It was also near impossible to put a telephone call through to the embassy in Moscow.[20]

36. *Arthur Whittall whose family had a long-established business in Istanbul. The itinerant Brian used him as a forwarding address.*

The Giffeys' patience was tested just once, in Odessa on the Black Sea, where they wanted to board a ship but were separated from their passports and luggage. Anni, normally shy and fearful, was so exasperated that she recalled a whole string of Russian swear-words her cousins had once taught her. "The only way to deal with the Russians is to shout at them and bully, and I did shout and was as rude as I knew how to be in Russian," she told her diary.

Christmas was spent on a comfortable Soviet ship that took them to Istanbul where they were met by Capt Arthur Whittall, the local passport control officer. Anni loved the city instantly "because almost every step you take in that enchanted town leads you to some beautiful view or interesting place." She had plenty of time to wander around while Brian was working at the embassy. Turkey was neutral but it was important to determine Russia's intentions, as the Germans were expected to advance to Iraq. Istanbul had become an important spy centre and it was no surprise that Brian was reunited with a few old friends.

Anni's time in Istanbul was filled with fun, laughter and dancing. Her duties were not onerous. "There was a Turk whom Brian had known in the Baltic, he used to call almost every day at the Pera Palace [their hotel] and as Brian was pretty busy, it fell to me to entertain him – the only common language we had was German. I had forgotten a great deal of mine and he had never known a lot. His main interest was language, the secrets of grammar and the birth of words, I'm afraid a subject which bored me to tears, but there we were day after day, smoking Turkish cigarettes (which I do not like), drinking Turkish coffee and making rather lame conversation in most terrible German."

37. The Pera Palace in Istanbul.

Chapter 8

Destination Baghdad

The Giffeys next journeyed to Iraq where they spent almost a week in Baghdad in February 1941. Not particularly attracted to the city and intent on getting to London, they could not possibly foresee that they would return to Baghdad in two years' time. The only available safe route in 1941 went through India, South Africa and Sierra Leone. They arrived in London in mid-April, just in time for the heaviest bombardments in the Blitz. The couple had read about the devastation the bombing had caused but there was still room for Anni to be shocked when confronted with reality. She was amazed at the Londoners' stoic acceptance of the noise and destruction; she quickly labelled them heroes.

Brian and Anni soon paid a visit to Claire, Brian's ex-wife, in Kent. A lyrical note crept into Brian's descriptions as they approached her home in Lenham on a beautiful spring day. Brian "started recognising Claire's trees, recognised them from the lovely white chalk cliffs, and then saw the workmen's cottages, and there, higher up, the chimney of her tiny cottage." It was a nice day for all three Giffeys (Claire had retained her married name after the divorce), with tea and cake taken on the lawn. All of them seem to have enjoyed the day. Brian and Anni were reunited with their favourite books, statuettes, silver, glass and Brian's prizes that had been left with Claire for safekeeping.

Brian and Anni's belongings were by now scattered all over the world. One of their trunks ended up in Chicago where Peter Gallienne was working as consul. The trunk had been sent from Tallinn to Helsinki, then onward to Lisbon, next to Brazil and Panama and finally, to the USA, in the belief that it belonged to Gallienne. When he opened it, Gallienne was disappointed because it turned out to be Brian's. "It contained your sword, a compass, a pocket range finder, some glassware (some broken), some clothes and a number of books," Gallienne told Brian. There was an oil painting of Gallienne, a portrait, that Brian had done in Tallinn, which the diplomat now extracted. "I also extracted two notebooks in your handwriting in Russian, and your own particular brand of shorthand. It seemed to me that to leave them with the Customs authorities here might either be dangerous or cause difficulties," he added wisely.[1]

Some of the Giffeys' belongings were later found intact under tarpaulin in the courtyard of the British embassy in Moscow, but some photographs lost in Helsinki were never recovered. When in 1950 Brian was invited to a wedding in London, he missed his top hat, although he had heard it was safe in Moscow. A shipment from Moscow did miraculously arrive in 1955 when they were in London, containing a lot of china and glass. "Anni worked all day very hard washing and stowing them. Now everything is beautifully put away and looks beautiful," Brian noted. The top hat was no longer important.

Back in 1941, another day off was spent with Nadja, the Russian who had been Brian's housekeeper and lover in Tallinn. She was now living in Bognor Regis and the Giffeys went to Victoria station to meet her train. "There she was.

Well dressed, but enormously fat and a terrifically loud voice. She greeted me tactfully as Brian Georgievich" in the Russian fashion, Brian remarked. She, like Claire, had become a fixture in Anni's life.

In London the Giffeys lived at the Estonian legation at 167 Queen's Gate for almost a year. Ernst Sarepera, the secretary and counsellor, had a largish flat on the premises. Recently separated, he had space to spare. Anni found the accommodation charming and was overwhelmed by the fact that the 7-storey building was still called the Estonian legation. "When I first saw the Estonian flag again after such a long time, my knees gave way," she said. The Estonian minister, August Torma, and his wife Alice invited the Giffeys to dinner and Alice Torma gave Anni knitting tips on how to start a pullover. Relations with Sarepera, however, temporarily withered over "servant trouble".

38. Former Estonian legation at 167 Queen's Gate, London, 2006 (now the embassy of Oman).

In her diary Anni devoted much space to the siblings she had left behind: her sisters Helmi (also known as Totti) and Hilja, niece Dagmar (Totti's daughter, aka Dagi) and brother Ants. No doubt because of Brian's influence, Anni adopted the habit of formulating written prayers. These included even Claire (aka Bee or Booshy) and Nadja. To a modern-day reader they may seem naive, but the times were uncertain and Anni was a young and immature woman. The following example was written when Estonia was under German occupation: "Dear God, save my beloved in Estonia so that they would have food, a roof overhead and clothes, so that they would not know fear. Dear God, you alone can help them. If it is your will, there might be some hope that we will meet up again one day. I can't even write, don't know where they are. Are they in Tallinn, in the countryside or deported to Russia or Germany? They have got so little out of life; Totti, Hilja and Dagi are so young, mother and father and Aunt Netty so old, and Ants has been working all his life – please help them.

"Dear God, please do so that the war would end, peace, happiness and silence descend on the world, Estonia be free again. Please help so that the millions would not suffer, poor soldiers would not be cut to pieces by bombs, bullets and bayonets, so that they would not have to die in pain far away from those who love them, so that women and children would not be homeless. You alone can help, even Bee who has been working all her life, dreamt of having a home, but not had a real home anywhere. And Nadja who is alone among strangers. I have Brian whom I love with all my heart. Please save him and help him so that he could do work that satisfies him. Help us so that we would stay together, even if we have to move away from here. Save me as well and help me gain more courage; help me so that I, too, could do my share of work for Britain and Estonia. You can help, dear God. Amen."

Brian's next posting was going to be in the Middle East. Iran was first mentioned in May 1941. Tehran had failed to provide military information about the Soviet-Iranian border area and the plan was to fly Brian in to rectify the situation. That, however, meant that Anni would stay behind, as wives were not allowed in Tehran. Brian disagreed. He insisted on Anni accompanying him wherever he was sent. In October Iran was confirmed and a way was paved for Anni to be trained so that she could go with him legitimately as a member of staff. She started work for one of Brian's bosses (referred to by the Giffeys confusingly as Bill or C) in Caxton Street, probably in SOE (Special Operations Executive). Ostensibly she was working for the Foreign Office. That her work was secret is evident from Brian's note about a dinner at which some friends had "tried very hard to find out where Anni works." One can only wonder where they thought that Brian was working.

Brian's office was at the MI6 headquarters in Broadway Buildings where he was put in charge of the stations in Sweden, Finland and the Soviet Union.[2] For 18 months he was section chief; this was promotion. His boss had obviously been satisfied with his work in Estonia. In London his focus didn't change much; he had become a Soviet specialist. The pre-war Estonian military intelligence chief, Richard Maasing, was an old friend. Now an émigré in Stockholm, Maasing had excellent if mysterious contacts and MI6 regarded his information highly. However, Maasing refused to name his sub-sources and London was concerned. So was Moscow because even in 1945 Maasing had two sub-agents in Estonia who were trusted members of the Communist Party and it was imperative to identify the men. Philby suggested that Maasing should be given an ultimatum, hoping thereby to pressure him into revealing the names, but Maasing refused and was therefore dropped as a British agent.[3]

SIS-Soviet relations had become complicated ever since the Soviets in 1941 became allies in the war. Brian had to achieve a balancing act. On the one hand a political decision had been taken to suspend all intelligence against Moscow, on the other there was a need for information about the Red Army. Alongside Maasing, another good source was Gen Makoto Onodera, the Japanese military attaché in Stockholm, whose Russian incidentally was much better than his English or German. This meant that he had time for Russian speakers. For the same reason he had also good Finnish contacts. Brian and Maasing remembered him from Kaunas, his previous attaché post. They had also met him in Tallinn.

Much valuable information came also from the Polish station in Stockholm that was cooperating with Scandinavian intelligence services.[4] Meanwhile direct links with Moscow remained difficult. There was concern in London that under the 1939 Nazi-Soviet agreement information had already travelled from Moscow to Berlin. A British mission was sent to Moscow to encourage mutually beneficial information exchanges, but Philby told the Soviets that SIS had neglected their country and received little information from Moscow. The latter was painfully true, and frustrating for London. Meanwhile SIS was bending over backwards in an effort to avoid revealing to the Soviets the code-breaking successes at Bletchley. The Soviets were not to know that the German communication codes had been cracked. However, Philby and John Cairncross seem to have sent highly secret information to the Russians all the same.[5]

Brian's own notes hardly mention work, except that he was writing his "magnum opus" in April and that kept him busy. One morning in August he left home at 0820 and worked all day, with a break for (a long?) lunch, had tea at the Estonian legation, then worked, saw his boss ("Big Brother") for an hour, had dinner and drinks and worked again until 4 am. This meant that by the following morning he had only had three hours' sleep before starting all over again.

It seems unusual to keep an officer in the head office once his field destination is known. Brian had time to take up Persian at SOAS, visit Bletchley Park and become a member of the Royal Central Asian Society. Was he being trained for something special while waiting? For about four months Brian and Anni were living at Abbots Langley near St Albans where Section V (counter-intelligence) was located. No doubt Brian familiarised himself with the unit working at the mansion called Glenalmond (now a children's nursery). Counter-intelligence had been a weak link in SIS operations up until then. Was it going to be Brian's focus in the Middle East? Was familiarisation with Section V the reason for keeping him in England? Or was there no-one else to take charge of the Soviet Union in Broadway Buildings?

Brian must have met Philby around that time, if not before. All three men – Brian, Frank Foley and Harry Steptoe – whom Philby named in *My Silent War*, as discussed in the introduction, were working at Section V in 1941-42 when Philby was there. The three were roughly the same age and each had had considerable field experience. So how did Philby come to form an unfavourable opinion of them? He was a young man, half their age, new to intelligence. Why did he think that these seasoned men were not good enough to train new recruits in sabotage and subversion?

All three men are known to have made anti-communist statements; they had a lively interest in current affairs and discussion. Their obvious distaste for communism must have been detected by Philby. If that was the reason for his dislike, the antipathy was probably mutual. At least Frank Foley's opinion of Philby is recorded, thanks to a colleague: "FF decided that Kim was to be avoided that evening. He already had his suspicions, or maybe I should say 'feelings', and during the course of the evening, he asked me – his words – 'How well do you know Philby?'. It was only later of course that I realised the significance of this remark."[6] Brian must have shared Foley's unease; he and Foley were close enough to have discussed Philby at some point.

Philby's charm worked well on another member of staff, Nicholas Elliott, who was a few years his junior. These two had attended the same college, drunk in the same bars, belonged to the same clubs, wore the same well-tailored clothes; they even learnt the spy trade together. Apart from Elliott, there were others who were equally charmed by Philby. "Even his senior officers recognised his abilities and deferred to him," a colleague, possibly Graham Greene, said.[7] Greene, who wrote a flattering introduction to *My Silent War*, said that he "had grown to like Kim immensely during the period when I worked with him in 1942-3" and called him "my friend" long after Philby had been unmasked as a Soviet spy. A biographer has suggested that the famous writer knew about Philby all along and even wondered whether Greene himself had passed secret information to the Soviets.[8]

Alfons Rebane, an Estonian who worked for Sandy McKibbin in London, issued words of warning about Soviet moles in the 1950s, without naming Philby, or anybody else for that matter. Rebane was bitter when the SIS Baltic operations came to a premature and sorry end because the Soviets had uncannily known in advance about the British agents' arrival and caught them there and then. As late as 1958 he suggested that SIS should "check out their own men and see how far the

Russian infiltration has gone – I fear that one day there might be huge surprises." Two years later, when Philby was not yet seriously suspected of working for the Soviets, Rebane noted that information had been leaked to the Russians "through the people at the top". He was altogether opposed to information sharing with Russia and thought that Estonia as a small nation had lost out in the deal.[9]

When in October 1942 the Giffeys finally set out for the Middle East their destination was no longer Tehran, but Baghdad. So much for Brian's Persian studies. There was altogether change in the air. Not only had the Soviets become allies, but the Germans were beaten at Alamein while the Giffeys were at sea. This was a crucial turning point in the war.

The journey to Baghdad was a reverse of 1941, only more complicated. The troopship The Empress of Scotland took two months from London to Durban because she sailed via Brazil. In Durban the couple boarded the Felix Russell that took them to Cairo. Anni was predisposed to like Cairo because Brian had spoken enthusiastically about its magic. She said the city stood for "romance mixed with rest and comfort". On a different level she enjoyed the evening spent in a fellow intelligence officer's home. "What a lovely flat they've got – for us wandering folk it was beautiful and comfortable," she said wistfully. "We love travel," she added quickly, "nothing could satisfy us more than going from place to place."

Brian spent most of his time in the office, but he was pleased to take Anni to places he remembered from 1914: the Citadel, the pyramids and the Ghezira sporting club. The club was something very special. "There I knew," Anni wrote of their visit, "that Brian was more homesick for his youth, for being again a soldier, than he has been anywhere else. It used to be

39. The Shepheard's Hotel, Cairo.

his club, he used to play polo – among the hundred ponies two used to belong to him personally." Anni admired Ghezira's beautiful lawns, the cool swimming pool and its location on a lovely island that had previously been the botanical gardens. Brian, too, looked back fondly on his pre-war period in Egypt: "I was often to think of it with nostalgia as my last experience of affluence and cultured ease before the difficulties, many anxieties and always interesting and often exciting events of the years to follow."

It would be fascinating, if it were possible, to compare the brief Brian was given in London in October 1942, before he set out for Baghdad, with what was discussed in Cairo in January 1943. So much had happened between those dates and this would impact on his intelligence work. The Giffeys spent nearly a month at the elegant Shepheard's Hotel, so there must have been things to discuss. Brian no doubt saw Capt Cuthbert

Bowlby, head of the Inter-Services Liaison Department (ISLD) and Col Raymond Maunsell, head of the Security Intelligence Middle East (SIME), both of whom had a coordinating function. Maunsell incidentally is said to have left some uncatalogued papers at the Imperial War Museum, but there is no trace of them at present.[10]

The last leg of the Giffeys' journey, a train to Baghdad, was uncomfortable and the carriage was dirty. Cleanliness mattered greatly to Anni. They arrived in Baghdad on 23 January 1943, so the journey from London had taken them exactly three months (with a month spent in Cairo). At around this time another major victory occurred at Stalingrad. It eliminated the threat of the Germans breaking through the Caucasus and fighting their way further south, into Iraq. By March Lt Gen Henry Pownall, the Allied commander-in-chief, was confident that the threat of a German land offensive was removed and an air attack unlikely.[11] This in effect meant that by the time the Giffeys arrived in Iraq the country was no longer in danger; it had become a backwater.

Iraq had been in turmoil before their arrival. A pro-German uprising had taken place in April 1941 led by the then Prime Minister Rashid Ali. He ousted the regent and seized power, but the British acted quickly, sent in Indian troops, occupied the country and so the period of open pro-Axis support was short-lived. The regent was restored to power, and the British continued to occupy the land. The Iraqi government was weak, there was a chronic wheat shortage and rampant inflation, and the Kurdish tribes in the north were restless. Also, Iraqi army loyalty was much in doubt. On the positive side Iraq belatedly, in January 1943, declared war on Germany and this news was welcomed in London. London also foresaw no fighting in Iraq unless Germany invaded Turkey.[12]

Anni quickly recalled their first visit to Baghdad. "Most people here hate this town," she said, "and I must say three years ago when we first passed through here I was terribly disappointed, as I always had imagined it quite romantically. Then everything looked drab and sand-coloured and dirty and the smells nearly knocked me down."[13] This time round it was the high cost of living that hit them. All the same, they quickly grew to like the place. "People think us crazy – Brian and me, that we say – we love Baghdad – but we do – really. It is lovely to get up in the morning and see blue sky round you – not a tiniest cloud anywhere," she told her diary, having seen enough grey skies elsewhere.

40. The Tigris, Baghdad, 1920.

For the first few months the Giffeys stayed at the Zia Hotel. When the embassy's first secretary, Harold Freese-Pennefather, celebrated his birthday, he invited the couple to the party. Brian was at work when Anni found that the violet evening dress with a brocade jacket that Brian had wanted her to wear needed ironing. "I did not dare to give them to be ironed in the bazaars – so I asked for an iron – they have an iron in the hotel, but it is too powerful for the fuses here – so twice I burnt them through – and still could not use the iron – so I spent the whole afternoon ironing my beautiful velvet dress on an ordinary [light] bulb – it took me hours, but the result was quite good." Waiting for Brian, who was delayed at the office, Anni had an unexpected Arabic lesson when Brian's teacher turned up and there was no Brian. All was well in the end; the party was enjoyable, there was champagne and a musical programme. The company was good as well: the Egyptian and Persian ministers, Mr and Mrs L. Pott, the British consul in Baghdad, Mr and Mrs W.L.C. Knight, the British consul-general in Basra and Mr and Mrs J. Walker, the embassy's commercial secretary.

Frequent parties and dinners were given by the core group of British ministerial people and wives. Some became personal friends (Mr C.R. Grice, assistant adviser at the Ministry of the Interior and deputy controller of censorship), some were good bridge partners, but others Anni did not take to at all. "Are all English women as stupid as that?" she wondered one evening. "They may be good women, but as soon as they open their mouths one wishes they would shut them again." Mrs Pott, the consul's wife, was an exception; Anni liked her.

There were days when Anni just wanted to draw into her shell. "I'm sometimes so tired of strange faces that I'd much rather stay in bed and read than entertain or be entertained, but we can't escape from them."[14] And there were cultural differences to consider. At one of the parties "a whole sheep was put on the table and men (mostly all were men except three women, me included) started tearing pieces off the roasted sheep with their dirty hands – well – I just could not stomach that yet," Anni admitted.

What was Brian doing in this quiet backwater? One of his tasks was to keep an eye on the comings and goings of dubious characters. Some were suspected of being German spies, who used railway conductors as couriers. Queries about particular individuals, often from the Combined Intelligence Centre Iraq (CICI), crossed Brian's desk at the embassy. For example, Werner Reist, the Swiss delegate of the International Red Cross, was travelling from Karachi to Geneva, with a stopover in Baghdad. He was known to have made disparaging remarks about the British and been in touch with Franz von Papen, the German ambassador to Turkey. In Iraq he was going to be under surveillance, as organised by Mr J.F. Wilkins of the Criminal Investigation Department.[15] Another person of interest was Ahmed Bahgat Bey, who had been appointed first secretary at the Egyptian legation in Baghdad and was known to have pro-Axis sympathies.[16] A Hungarian spy, Gyula Kovacs, who had lived in Baghdad before the war and was now working for the Germans in Istanbul and Sofia, was said to have Iraqi agents yet to be identified.[17]

Intercepted letters were translated as a matter of course, many of them seemingly innocuous. Consider this one, for example: "I am in good health. I am sending you my photo to show you my health and condition. Please convey my best wishes to father and mother and to all the family. You can send your letter either to my address in Istanbul or to Manisa, as I have previously instructed you." Letters of this kind enabled the British to keep track of Iraqi refugees and their movements in Turkey.[18] Many of them were "Iraqi undesirables" and it was best to keep them in neutral Turkey, even if they requested exit visas. Various delays could be conveniently invented.[19] After all, Rashid Ali and his friends, who had pulled off the coup in 1941, were still at large, thought to be in Germany. And German radio propaganda – "Berlin in Arabic" and "Voice of Free Arabism" – continued to be broadcast (although few in

Iraq had radio receivers – only 4,000, as opposed to 55,000 in Egypt).

There was interest in Ahmad Hilmi Ibrahim of the Egyptian legation because he was corresponding with "my dearest Marta". The man had previously been in Italy and was suspected of being an Axis sympathiser. He had been successfully using the consular privilege for his correspondence, so that letters were actually posted in Cairo, but a small mistake in the arrangement allowed the censor to conclude that the letters were in fact destined for enemy territory and that Marta had been writing in German.[20]

And then there were the Soviets to consider. SIS was beginning to look ahead to the end of the war. Having previously suspended all anti-Soviet activities, SIS wanted to know what the Soviets were up to now that the war was going to be won. What were their post-war intentions? The Soviets were allies but they could not be fully trusted. Geographically they were close by – they had occupied northern Iran and a fully-functioning Soviet embassy had been set up in Tehran (the one in Baghdad only opened after Brian's departure in 1944) but its diplomats were said to be operating in splendid isolation. Contacts were badly needed to gain access and information. Czechs and Poles had been useful in the past, and Brian revived his Polish contacts from Tallinn.

Tens of thousands of Poles had flooded into Iraq after their release from Soviet labour camps in 1941. They expected to be part of the Polish Army in the East under Gen Wladislaw Anders. Polish uniforms were frequently sighted in Baghdad, Anni's diary mentions Polish concerts and art exhibitions, and there was a Polish mission in town.

Lt-Col Tadeusz Rudnicki was one of the Poles Brian knew from Tallinn. He had arrived from Kaunas to evacuate Polish military internees whom the pro-Moscow Estonians had detained in their eagerness to please their new Soviet masters. Brian met Rudnicki again in Jerusalem in July 1943 when the Pole was on his way to Tehran to take up his post as military attaché. Previously he had been an attaché in Moscow where he had worked closely with British intelligence.[21] Rudnicki had also accompanied Gen Wladislaw Sikorski, head of the Polish government-in-exile, during the latter's visit to Iraq in May 1942.

Another visit by Gen Sikorski was expected in 1943. Brian must have been involved in some way because he made a cryptic note (misspelling Sikorski's name) when the general was on his way to Iraq: "Szikorski in Italy. With all this visit (with ref.ce to Anders) I may have helped – thanks to W."

When Brian and Rudnicki met in Jerusalem, Brian hoped that the Pole would put him in touch with authoritative Polish sources in Iraq. For this purpose Brian asked London to provide a questionnaire to specify the subjects on which complete and authoritative information was required.[22] This detail is known thanks to historian Gill Bennett. It suggests that at least some of Brian's communications with London have survived somewhere in the depths of MI6 archives. Another of Brian's Polish contacts was Jozef Przeslowski of whom only name is known. He visited the Giffeys' home in Baghdad in January 1944.

Another, frequent, visitor was Capt Edwardes who had a (Russian or Georgian) wife in Tbilisi. Reginald Wharry and Stan Sedcole were important visitors from Tehran who stayed for a week at a time. Anni liked both men and was pleased to hear that Sedcole's wife was Estonian. The two men came to Baghdad because SIS officers were keeping an eye on the movements of Soviet officials. This required cooperation between Tehran and Baghdad because "all movements of Soviet official and unofficial personnel from the Tehran zone to the British zone in this country [Iran] and also to Iraq and Egypt are communicated by the VM [vice-minister?] in Tehran to the VM in Baghdad and to the SIS head of station in Tehran before permission for the journey is given." This meant that there was information available about Soviet movements, but it was often limited, not revealing enough. Tehran and Baghdad needed to identify individuals but often only surnames were known, sometimes an initial as well, but no first name. Often the job title was missing.[23]

Meanwhile it was known that the largest Soviet intelligence presence abroad was in Tehran where the Soviets had an agency of 115 officers. Their main task was to identify, abduct and liquidate persons whom Stalin had deemed to be anti-Soviet.[24] Thanks to the Cambridge Five, the Soviets were well-informed about the thinking in London and fully aware of British concerns. They had seen, for example, the British Joint Intelligence Sub-Committee report of 15 February 1943 and concluded: "The entire paper is testimony to a fear of the Red Army's success and the growth of the Soviet Union's influence."[25]

There were also the local Iraqi communists to consider. They cleverly used the high cost of living and bread and flour shortages in their propaganda. "There is now a well-established and popular left wing daily newspaper [called Al-Qaeda, meaning The Base], which makes a feature of news and articles favourable to Russia," the ambassador, Sir Kinahan Cornwallis, told London. Recent Soviet military successes helped the communists' cause. Many Iraqi communists were ill-disposed towards Britain, argued in favour of diplomatic relations with the Soviet Union and were agitating "to belittle the Allied help given to Russia and to stress the point that the Communists are as determined as any other Arab political group to carry on the struggle for full independence of all Arab countries."[26] The Iraqi communist party was banned, but it operated illegally until a raid and arrests in 1943 paralysed it for a while. However, its leader Comrade Fahd then returned from Moscow where he had stayed for six months, and rebuilt the organisation.[27]

41. Al-Rashid Street, central Baghdad, 1940.

By March 1943 the Giffeys had moved into Stewart Perowne's bungalow right in the heart of Baghdad. Perowne, a promising young man, was the public relations attaché at the embassy. Brian thought he was intelligent and brilliantly witty but to Anni he seemed "a bit of an eccentric". However, the house was nice, its six rooms were fully furnished and the garden was beautiful. During the first few days Anni spent her mornings selecting and cutting the best roses, and arranging them in vases. She enjoyed the novelty of it; she had not had a garden before. The house came with a full complement of house servants and a gardener, but they caused no end of trouble for Anni. The boys had no concept of honesty, she concluded. "You have to lock up everything, and even then they pinch things. Not a lot at once, but small things and in small quantities. Specially food. So everything has to be given out in small quantities – I hate not trusting people – but one just can't do anything else here."[28] The Giffeys also employed a driver, but it was the succession of unsatisfactory cooks that made most impact on the household.

The summer heat was unpleasant, to put it mildly, and there were scorpions. Nine had been killed by September. Anni was told never to relax: walking barefoot, even in the bathroom, was not a good idea, just in case. "Before you go to bed you have to look between your sheets and under your pillows – because people have found them there and [you] have to shake out your clothes and shoes always before putting them on. And [there are] huge spiders – not tarantulas but sort of salmon-coloured ones the size of your fist. Disgusting-looking creatures. I'm much more frightened of the spiders than scorpions, because they move with such terrific speed. Some people say they are poisonous, others – they are not."

"But life is pleasant here in the city of Sheherezade and the caliphs," she continued dreamily. "We live luckily in a sort of bungalow suburb, and when you sit in your garden which is completedly isolated with oleander bushes you can imagine that you are in England. Beautiful lawns, flowers, trees and the peace of a sleepy suburban place – only doves or pigeons and sparrows and at night a full chorus of frogs."[29]

On another day, in a different mood, she wrote: "I should hate to live all my life in the East. You get here everything and you do very little yourself, having servants to do all the work, but there is something lacking. Life here is artificial."

Much of her joy was derived from pets. "Dear me, our family is growing rapidly," she chuckled. "Yesterday I got a little bulbul, that is now two cats and a bird and a frog. I am so sorry for the little bird. Has to stay in a cage. I dare not let her loose here, as there is fire in the fire-place and she may burn herself." When one of the cats, the black-and-white Tornado, "really sweet" and "so cute", fell ill, Anni devoted a page and a half of her diary to describing his condition. The cat died shortly after. "Both Brian and I feel bloody – wherever we go Tornado is missing."

Four spies – three Germans and an Iraqi – parachuted into the Mosul area in June and were caught soon after. The men wore civilian, Kurdish-style clothes and were carrying Kurdish national emblems. Preliminary questioning was carried out by the British in Baghdad. It was established that the agents' primary object had been to incite Kurds to action against the Allies, but there was no apparent evidence of sabotage plans. A secondary objective may have been to gather information about Allied strength and movements. A specialist officer from SIME, Security Intelligence Middle East, arrived from Cairo to question the men and one of the spies, Gottfried Müller, confessed.

The Iraqis wanted the spies court martialled; meanwhile the Swiss consul, representing German interests, was knocking on the British embassy door in the hope of talking to the men. Sir Kinahan Cornwallis, the ambassador, was away all summer and the chargé d'affaires, Geoffrey Thompson, was temporarily in charge. He asked London for advice and was told: "No objection need be raised to prisoners being treated as spies." However, there was also a warning: "So long as Iraqis do not allow them to escape and they have a proper trial, it does not matter whether they are tried by court martial or in ordinary courts, but it would be most undesirable for an execution of a death sentence to follow immediately after the trial before there was time for further consideration." As to the Swiss consul, London said, he had no legal standing and if the British military security authorities decided he should be denied facilities, their decision was final.[30]

Thompson, however, felt snubbed that the SIME specialist who came to interrogate the spies "never had the courtesy to call on me." The man had been ignorant "about the political set-up in this country and had to have explained to him in words of one syllable just what we can and what we can't do in the way of ordering the Iraqis about." This made Thompson congratulate his embassy and the Iraqis (the interior minister and the police chief) on developing friendly relations so that "the initial squabbling... gave place to complete acquiescence in all the requests made from our side."[31]

His choice of word – "squabbling" – makes one wonder why Nigel Clive wanted to discuss rivalries in the Baghdad chapter of his memoirs; his book otherwise centres on Greece. Clive was new to intelligence and, while in Baghdad, wanted to understand how the secret service worked. There were a number of different organisations in Baghdad. What he found amounted to constant bickering and jealousy between MI6, MI5 and SOE. He admitted becoming "cynical about the time spent on fierce interdepartmental warfare. It became a commonplace to say that if fifty per cent of the day could be devoted to trying to defeat Hitler, we were doing well and might win the war. The SOE team was unquestionably the best in my view and I collaborated with them closely. This did not always please the head of my office (SIS), who preferred to believe what he was told by his own sources of information, and had restricted his contacts with the rest of the intelligence community to an irreducible minimum."[32]

But who was this unidentified head of office? Was it Brian? Clive has just said that the head of Baghdad station came to recruit him in Sarafand, near Jerusalem, in the summer of 1941. The year is confirmed by the official MI6 history, so it must be correct. Clive's description of the recruiter – "a middle-aged figure of military bearing" – fits Brian but is far too vague for identification. Nigel West, on the other hand, had no doubt that Clive was recruited by Brian Giffey (although he called him Frank). However, Brian was in London at the time of this recruitment, working as section chief. It is possible that he flew in from London, but unlikely that he would have stayed long enough to look for an assistant to analyse the political situation in the aftermath of the Rashid Ali rebellion, as Clive has said. Brian and Anni had already spent a week in Baghdad earlier that year, in February, when travelling from Tallinn to London, but the Rashid Ali coup took place in April. That makes it unlikely that Brian was the recruiter in the summer of 1941.

Clive has further complicated matters by saying that his boss, the recruiter, left after a year (it can't have been Brian who had not even arrived by 1942) and his replacement, "another major from the First World War, lasted a matter of months. When he left in the early summer of 1943, our regional head office in Cairo asked me to take over the Embassy intelligence organization and offered me promotion. They seemed aggrieved when I turned down the job." At that stage Clive joined SOE instead.[33] This sequence of events cannot be right because it leaves Brian completely out of the picture. There is no room for him in Clive's memoirs.

Clive also says that there were two SIS representatives in Baghdad: No 1, the head of station, and No 2, his assistant, i.e. Clive himself. The official history of MI6, however, refers to a "sole representative" who had "fourteen agents, three of whom (reflecting the strategic importance of Iraqi and Iranian oil) were dedicated to Ministry of Economic Warfare work." The station, set up in 1939, was the smallest in the Middle East, it says.[34] Anni, by the way, kept a diary in Baghdad but it rather adds to the confusion. She mentions Andy Clive, while the man's full name was Nigel David Clive. More smoke and mirrors?

There is no doubt that Brian Giffey arrived in Baghdad in January 1943 and left in May 1944 and between those dates he was the head of station (82000). In Baghdad, like in Tallinn, Brian was awarded the local rank of second secretary. Something about the arrangement, however, niggled and the relationship between him and the embassy staff was "far from good".[35] Brian was too much of an independent spirit to behave like a diplomat at all times, and this may have been resented in some quarters. Consider, for example, the comment made about one of Brian's (nameless) successors: "He is on the Diplomatic List as a Second Secretary and I have never raised any objection to this because he is, in my opinion, an admirably discreet person who does not throw his weight around and remains as far as possible in the background."[36] Brian, alas, was not background material.

The embassy can't have been a happy place. A visiting MI6 agent, Harry Steptoe, filed interesting observations: "The Oriental secretary [Capt Vyvyan Holt] apparently has a dim view of SIS, shared to a lesser degree by the counsellor [Geoffrey Thompson], who apparently has leftist leanings. As a result of this, and possibly other factors too, for the Oriental secretary's office to be providing the cover for ISLD (Inter-Services Liaison Department [MI6]) may be rather unreliable." Steptoe went on to give a damning account of Stewart Perowne, the clever public relations attaché, who clearly did not approve of MI6 working on embassy premises. Perowne's "direct aim is reputed to be to sabotage the SIS station in Baghdad, on the grounds that its use of writing and paid Iranian agents is incompatible, in his opinion, with his work as a public relations officer," Steptoe remarked. London had been told that Perowne was trying "to penetrate SIS through one of the radio operators attached to our station" and was keeping the company of British men (he was homosexual) who were "ideologically sympathetic to Communism."[37]

Perowne's communist tendencies were also observed by Brian, who said that Perowne "was anything but a democrat or a friend of the People whom it was his ambition in life to help to enslave to that sabre-toothed tiger, Stalin – in Britain and throughout the world." Perowne was "typical of a type who took to Communism eagerly, as offering the answer to all problems," he said.

42. Former British legation in Baghdad, 1915.

The embassy was located in a handsome Ottoman mansion right on a bank of the Tigris. Anni knew it well. She befriended some of Brian's office staff; they were on first-name terms.

"Aubrey and Nora came to see us and he brought us again some cigarettes. He is a nice boy," Anni said in June 1943. By September, however, the "nice boy" had caused much headache. "Aubrey has stolen a lot of money in the time we've been here. Now he's gone and Brian has got a lot of mess to clear up... So one way or another there has been trouble everlasting. I do hope for Brian's sake that it will be cleared up soon. The heat, and understaffed as he is, [this] is not good for him," Anni told her diary. Brian had a terribly worrying time at the office, she said. Brian echoed her thoughts when he wrote: "I've had the hardest time I've ever had with Aubrey's dishonesty, my chief's disapproval, single-handed, a completely inexperienced staff, the heat, so much to do, the terrible feeling that I'm not getting on with it, nothing but administration, not a report got off for a fortnight (!)."

The Giffeys may have found the situation, even the difficult summer heat, easier to manage if Anni had been working. She had after all been trained in London before they left for Baghdad. Or had she? Little is known about the nature of her work/training: it lasted for eleven months and involved typing. She had previously helped out at the embassies in Tallinn and Helsinki where she had taught herself to type and may have also acquired rudimentary shorthand. The 1941-42 period in London, however, was the longest that she ever worked and it was not easy. Perhaps the training plan failed?

Anni, however, frequently told her diary how busy she was. Early on she mentioned the Red Crescent, for example, and said: "I have to go to a committee meeting today." She wanted to make a good impression, but felt unsure. "I'm rather scared. I hope I won't disappoint these people." A later entry, however, suggests it had been just a ladies' tea party, not really a committee meeting, Anni had sensed intrigue and disliked the atmosphere. Elsewhere she has said, "I started my work already some time ago," but this seems to refer to visiting Iraqi ladies and being nice to them. She also taught English to some local children. "I always wanted to help the poor and now I've got the chance. I know it is going to be very interesting," she wrote in August.[38]

The complex tribal network fascinated Anni. She marvelled at the contrast between the sheikhs – some uncouth, some dignified – they had met in Basra. "Our host of the night before was an upstart nasty piece of work who tried to imitate Europeans and did it in a cheap way – our host [tonight], the sheikh, had all the grace and dignity of a people whose culture is much older than ours, whose family traditions go back for centuries... What a magnificent library he has – over 7,000 copies – some of them, quite a large number, are hand-written books." Getting to know the country was part of Brian's job, and this kept the couple occupied. "This week is going to be even worse," Anni said, "as we are going away for a week or ten days – up North, new country again – and I'm busy instructing the gardener, doing all sorts of odd jobs and Red Cross work and dancing with troops and playing bridge with the local ladies here and learning Arabic and goodness only knows what else. Also there are so many dinner parties that you have hardly a minute to yourself."[39]

One evening just two guests came, Neil Hogg, the embassy's second secretary, and Sheikh Abdul Qadir Bashayani from Basra. "It was to start with a bit heavy going," Anni wrote, "as the Sheikh does not speak English well and Hogg does not speak any Arabic. Neither do I, and Brian very little. The dinner made things easier. The Sheikh gave Brian a beautiful amber cigar-holder. He has also sent us a huge box of dates. After dinner we played cameroons. When they left I gave them our last roses." When the Giffeys went to Basra the sheikh took them to his house in a launch. Anni was impressed by his seven dogs (two of them beautiful Alsatians, she said) and the lovely big garden where among other plants she saw green roses.

"Last night we had dinner with [former government minister] Ibrahim Kamal and his wife," Anni wrote on another day. "They are very charming people and have a beautiful home. I felt quite homesick when I saw this well-looked-after home. Our home is charming, but not beautiful. It is so difficult to make it beautiful with the very scrappy furniture we've got here. Still, we are very lucky to have even what we've got."

Having met and liked the Arabist Freya Stark, Anni felt a need to justify their own mode of travel. "I do enjoy our trip here in the North – of course Freya Stark or anyone really experienced traveller would look with contempt at our way of travel. Always staying with Europeans and going by car instead of by mule or donkey and putting up at night in a karavanserai. But for their kind of trips one has to have time and leisure. We have limited time and it is a trip because Brian has to do it – not because we are here on holiday."

There was much tribal trouble, Kurdish in particular, in the country. The Iraqi government's answer was to quell uprisings and arrest tribal leaders. The British, keen to avoid serious involvement, took on the role of a middleman: they told the Kurds to be patient and asked the Iraqis to be more responsive. Tribal areas had after the 1941 coup acquired British political advisers who were doing their own mediation, but their representations, however, were not always benefiting the British cause because they had been living locally, knew the country well and had often more sympathy for the Kurds than the embassy in Baghdad.[40]

Mulla Mustafa, the Barzani chieftain in northern Kurdistan, escaped from detention in July 1943 and caused alarm by successfully raiding a number of police posts in September. An entire garrison surrendered to him in October. Talks were hastily organised but they produced no results.[41] The ambassador called Mustafa a bandit, resigned himself to "endemic restlessness in the Barzan area of Kurdistan", but maintained that the Iraqis must resolve their own problems. He reminded the prime minister, Nuri Pasha Said, "that for 20 years British officials have striven to help Government to consolidate their control over Kurdish areas. When concessions for Kurds have been advised aim has always been to reconcile them to their position in Iraq."[42]

London was pleased that Cornwallis was seeking no more than tranquillity and status quo by trying to avoid British military commitment. "We would certainly prefer not to become more deeply involved than is strictly necessary," the Foreign Office said. "Provided that the Mullah's successes against the Iraqi Government do not threaten other important British interests, e.g. our lines of communication, it would seem that actual operations against Mustafa should be left to the Iraqi Government, as being responsible for maintenance of internal order."[43]

"Our lines of communication" included the uninterrupted flow of Lend-Lease aid to Russia via Iraq and Iran. The aid sent to Russia was mostly military (tanks, guns, chemicals, explosives) but there was also food (American canned pork, egg and milk powder) and medication (e.g. penicillin, not known in the country before).[44] Russia was short of many things, and the quantities of aid were increasing. "From a total of 55,621 tons in March 1943, deliveries reached the figure of 178,617 tons in July, the highest yet reached," Lt-Gen Pownall reported.[45] "Our lines of communication" also included security for all-important oil.

Brian was out of action some of the time because he developed health problems. Bad stomach pains in February and March were followed by a diagnosis in late March: he had gallstones. In May he was sent to Bir Yakov near Jerusalem for an operation. Anni accompanied him and stayed at a nearby farm, visiting him every day at the 23rd British Hospital. The operation was successful: Brian's gallbladder was removed. This period, however, was a trial for Anni. Her diary is full of worry and more worry, thoughts that her beloved husband might die.

Two weeks after the operation when Brian was at last allowed to get up, Anni's patience snapped. She ran off in a huff once it was clear the hospital staff didn't need her help. Brian tried to reason with her in a note he sent. "I'm in a military hospital as an outsider, we are together on sufferance, we are treated with a kindness and consideration which, I assure you, are so unusual as to be quite exceptional." He asked her to remember "the millions of British wives alone whose husbands are fighting overseas – think of the hundreds of thousands, who bid their husbands farewell with a brave smile – who will never see them again." Anni had been selfish, he said. They had their future to consider. "That my health lasted all these years, that I was able to finish all my important work, that I didn't have another attack before the operation, that I got that wonderful week [before the operation] to get fit in, that the operation and the first part of the convalescence went so well and that with God's blessing I may look forward to many years of life and perfect health – and useful work, seems just a miracle for which we should never cease to thank God."

Chapter 9

Dismissed from intelligence service

September 1943 was difficult for the Giffeys. Brian was under much pressure and there was "never, never sleep enough!". He left Anni a bad-tempered note. "It's as if the devil possessed you to wake me up or keep me awake. If I have a breakdown, or my health gives way in any other way, we are ruined – for ever. So for God's sake, let me sleep today, don't don't worry me, let me do as I like, for God's sake! I'm near the end of my tether."

The couple had money worries. Iraq was altogether more expensive than they had expected. "I do wish I could get some money somehow," Anni told her diary, "we are in such desperate need of it. Brian needs his suits, I need my teeth seen to and so it goes on and there is no money – it is really terrible."

There was also the question of Brian's job security. "The business in the office has also shrivelled to a skeleton staff. Brian does not think that we will remain here for very long," she wrote in July. In October she hoped "that we can stay about another 2 months or so here." In February 1944 she observed that "Brian is very happy. He loves his job and we are very much in love." Barely three weeks later, however, a thunderbolt struck: "Brian got the sack today. We are to leave here in just over a month's time. I'm still quite dazed. We don't quite know what is going to happen to us in future – what Brian's future, or mine for that matter, activities will be. It all was presented in a very crude form and my dearest is so terribly hurt and unhappy... I'm certain that he'll find another job and perhaps it is all for the best. Perhaps it is a good thing he gets out of this crowd. There has always been such a lot of jealousy among them and they don't know who is a good man."

Anni was also worried about her family in Estonia. Fighting in 1944 was getting closer to the Estonian-Russian border and there were days when Anni didn't dare to follow the news. "I'm so terribly unhappy today – so depressed. I just wish I could go somewhere and hide myself and cry and cry and cry. They are fighting in Narva – Ah, please, please, dear God, help my people. Don't let them suffer. You can protect them and help them. Give them please courage and hope in a hopeless situation. You alone can do it. I know that my unhappiness cannot help them, but you can. Please help them. Amen."[1]

A colleague from Istanbul, Harold Gibson ("Gibby"), brought good news. Harry Carr, the station head in Stockholm, had told him that Anni's brother Ants had arrived safely in Sweden. He had had a spat with a German propaganda officer in Estonia and, fearing arrest, had fled. In Stockholm he was staying with Sandy McKibbin and work had been found for him at the US embassy. Anni was pleased that one of her flesh and blood was at last out in the free world.

As to their own future, Anni wrote defiantly: "But we are tough and we're quite used not to have a home. Hotels, boarding homes, trains and ships have been so long our lot that a real home is just a sweet ache – some time, somewhere on the cliffs of Wales, by the sea is our dream cottage, with a garden round it and a little yacht. Nobody can rob us of our dreams, and dreams keep you going, they give you resistance to shoulder all difficulties and sorrows."[2]

Brian was no stranger to hardship. "Every step I won was the reward of bitter struggle, made under severe handicaps, fighting grievous difficulties – one might have said: insurmountable obstacles – and serious prejudice, sometimes determined opposition and, on a few occasions, bitter hostility. Enthusiasm much more than ambition carried me through, enthusiasm and keenness on the job-in-hand. Good work began to attract for its own sake – the soldier, the intelligencer, the student and the public servant and yes, the athlete."

After his sacking Brian continued to work as if nothing had happened. Col John Teague, intelligence controller for the Middle East, and Michael Ionides, defence security officer in Beirut, came to visit in March. They were accompanied by a general whose name Anni did not catch. Anni thought that Ionides "is nice and one can talk sense to him." He had played host to the Giffeys in Beirut and had stayed with them in Baghdad in September. No previous contact with Teague has been recorded. The visit may have had something to do with Brian's dismissal.

The office staff were sad to see Brian go. As the news spread, Reginald Wharry, Brian's counterpart in Tehran, commiserated: "I am indeed sorry to hear you are not only leaving Baghdad but the firm as well. Whatever the reason there are ways of doing things, and HQ do not seem to have the happy knack of doing them gracefully."[3] Interestingly, enough correspondence has survived to suggest dissatisfaction with Wharry's own work, but there was no talk of dismissal – he was allowed to stay in post.[4] Brian thought his own "changed circumstances" were "due perhaps to a tactless presentation and insistence on my views, which is not always popular; though other matters will have complicated things for me."[5] In his proposed memoirs, the ones he never wrote, he planned to have a whole chapter entitled "The blow fell in Baghdad". Unless MI6 opens its archive, we will never know. However, we can speculate.

Espionage literature seems thin on dismissals. When Harry Steptoe behaved erratically in China in 1931, the British minister, Sir Miles Lampson, suggested that "we could abolish him altogether". Steptoe was told to explain himself to Adm Sir Hugh Sinclair, the head of MI6, and was subsequently advised to take sick leave, but he was not sacked. It was only in 1944 that Kim Philby engineered Steptoe's dismissal, but even that was probably described as retirement.[6] Graham Greene came close to dismissal in 1944 but was saved by Philby and resigned a few months later.[7] Philby himself "was retired from intelligence work", not dismissed, when suspicions arose about him working for the Soviets.[8] Brian by contrast was sacked on the spot, without even being recalled to London. What kind of error would merit that? It must have been something major. Telegrams must have flown between Baghdad and London, but somebody in authority had to deliver the verdict to Brian. Who had this authority?

The messenger could have been the ambassador, Sir Kinahan Cornwallis, whose duties included chairing weekly meetings attended by all intelligence and security branches in Baghdad. His link was with the Combined Intelligence Centre in Iraq (CICI), which some sources say was MI5.[9] Sir Kinahan enjoyed considerable authority and had at his disposal large amounts of money that the Foreign Office called the "fund for bribery and other secret activities," out of which, for example, as much as £7,200 was drawn in just a single month, August 1944, with Foreign Office approval.[10]

*43. Kinahan Cornwallis played an important part in the 1921
coronation of King Faisal I. From left: Sir Percy Cox (the British
high commissioner), Col Kinahan Cornwallis, Tahsin Qadri
(Faisal's aide-de-camp), Faisal and Sir Aylmer Haldane (the British
commanding officer). Col Cornwallis was knighted in 1929.*

Or the messenger could have been Cuthbert Bowlby, head
of the ISLD, representing MI6 in the Middle East. He might
have come all the way from North Africa to dismiss Brian.
The documents I have seen suggest, however, that Brian was
appointed by London and therefore any dismissal should have
also come from London. It is known that the MI6 representative
in Tehran "serves the local British authorities in Persia and is
directly under MI6 London."[11] In this case Brian, too, would
have been directly under MI6 London. And the chief who was
dissatisfied with him ("my chief's disapproval") in September
1943 would have been in London. So why was Brian not called
to London for dismissal?

It is even possible that Sir Kinahan might have initiated the
dismissal although Brian was representing MI6. Let us turn

to Philby for a helpful explanation: "The powers of the SIS representatives abroad are severely limited. The station head is under the control of the Minister or Ambassador, and the latter can always limit the activities of the SIS representative if he judges them to be politically dangerous." This suggests that Sir Kinahan was Brian's boss ("my chief") in Baghdad. Philby has also said that the SIS representative can protest to his section head if he disagrees with the minister or ambassador and the section head may take the matter to the permanent under-secretary of state for foreign affairs. "Unless the case for the SIS is overwhelmingly strong, it is obvious that the Foreign Office will support a cautious Ambassador rather than a vigorous SIS representative."[12] Can Philby, however, be trusted?

As to the reasons for Brian's dismissal, was there anything he had misjudged? He knew his reports were not liked by the Foreign Office. Even his style was disliked because he wrote "clearly, boldly and strongly", perhaps even "racily", and used slang. He had worried about the first of his Mosul reports and wondered "about my reports about Iran-Kurdistan and the Persian Gulf that were so unpopular." Could reporting style, however, lead to dismissal? If the reports were to blame they would have contained views, not just style, that were unacceptable. And what views might have been unacceptable? Something about the Kurdish situation, for example? Did Brian disagree with Sir Kinahan? Both men were of mature years and entrenched views; both knew the country well. Sir Kinahan was an Arabic speaker whom one of the British political advisers labelled a "dyed-in-the-wool Arabist", unable to see the Kurdish point of view.[13]

Could Brian's statements have been regarded as treason? A threat to this end had run through a circular issued by Col Wood who had warned his CICI staff to avoid making adverse comments on the policy of the Baghdad embassy. Adverse comments, he admonished, would amount to criticism of the policy of His Majesty's Government and that would be treason.[14] He was referring to talk among British officials who blamed London for Iraqi administrative inefficiency and corruption. In the event, is it possible that Brian said something in support of the Kurds that amounted to treason?

He must have discussed Iraq with the Estonian Gen Johan Laidoner while in Tallinn. Both men knew the country when it was still Mesopotamia. Brian had spent over a year there in 1917-18 and Laidoner had been appointed to adjudicate on the Iraqi-Turkish border by the League of Nations in 1925. As a result of Laidoner's report on this complex matter, the League decided to apportion the Mosul area to Iraq, not Turkey. The decision was very much welcomed by London while

44. *Colonel Johan Laidoner in 1919.*

leaving the Turks unhappy. Now, years later, Brian may have seen the weakness of some of the then arguments. He discussed Iraq's history and the British role with his wife, but Anni found much of it beyond her comprehension: "We've talked these last two days so much about these eastern countries, what Britain has done, what she should have done and what she could have done. It is all such a muddle in my head. I wish I could talk about these problems to some Iraqi – a broadminded man."[15]

In Brian's intended memoirs one of the chapters was going to be called "Fate waited at Mosul". It preceded the chapter on his dismissal, suggesting that something happened at Mosul that led to his downfall. Alas, the chapter heading is all there is – just these four words.

Might Brian's dismissal have had something to do with SIS reorganisation in London and plans for Section IX? The very same Steptoe, who in 1931 got off lightly by taking sick leave, was sent on an inspection tour of the Mediterranean stations in 1944 and visited Baghdad at the time when Brian was on the point of leaving. Steptoe's job was to check that the stations were paying enough attention to London's memo on Soviet security structures because of the renewed interest in Soviet post-war intentions. This renewed interest was behind the abolition of Section V and reactivation of Section IX.

Is it possible that Kim Philby, freshly appointed to head Section IX, engineered Brian's dismissal? If he arranged for Steptoe to be sacked and gloated about this in his memoirs, he may have done the same for Brian. It is only the matter of timing that is in question here. Work on reactivating the unit started in 1943 (Jeffery's official history makes Section IX live as early as May 1943) and Philby became the section head in "early" 1944.[16] Brian Giffey was dismissed on 25 February. So it is not impossible. But what about the motive? I would suggest that Philby, having scrutinised Brian's Estonian network of agents and betrayed it to Moscow, thought that the man, an anti-communist, might constitute a threat to him and should go. Or is it too far-fetched? I have no evidence other than Philby's unaccountable dislike of Brian. Also, Philby's own pro-Arab sympathies may have come into play.

Whatever the mechanics of Brian's dismissal, the Giffeys were back in England in July 1944, homeless and jobless. They were taken in by their Estonian friend Asta Jakobson who lived in West Byfleet, Surrey. The ambassador August

Torma, his wife Alice and the counsellor Ernst Sarepera were frequent visitors, staying to dinner and playing bridge. Anni spent much time knitting and Brian enjoyed sketching. All the same, he was worried about his work prospects, and even with hindsight he noted: "Summer 1944 was a fair warning, how insecure were future employment, earning power, position."

The war was drawing to a close. For Britain that meant looking forward, making plans for the post-war administration of Germany. Meanwhile Estonia, still under German occupation, worried about the approaching Soviet troops. Fears of a second Soviet occupation were widespread. As the Germans pulled out of the country in September, the Estonians seized the opportunity and set up a national government. However, they badly needed outside help to make it last. Capt Evald Jakobson, Asta's husband, acted as a courier in bringing the Estonian appeal to Torma in London, but there was nothing the ambassador could do.[17] The would-be Estonian government barely managed to tell the world of its existence before it fell and the Soviets took over. There was, however, a gap between the Germans departing and the Soviets arriving, and tens of thousands of Estonians took advantage of this to flee to the West.

Among those who fled to Sweden were several members of the Oras family. Anni's mother, sisters Totti and Hilja, and niece Dagi found themselves in refugee camps, knitting furiously to earn some money. Anni's brother Ants Oras had been safe in Stockholm for a year, but he was dissatisfied with his life as a "radio listener" for the Americans. Having specialised in English literature, he felt that his talents were wasted in this job; he wanted to go to England, if only for a visit. It was only natural to ask for his brother-in-law's help. This visa request must have been difficult for Brian to handle. He had

*45. Alexander
"Sandy" McKibbin.*

not told Ants about his dismissal, presumably expecting the news to filter through via their mutual friend Sandy McKibbin. Now that Ants sought his help, he had to tell him that he was powerless – he was no longer with SIS.

This still left another avenue to try – the Foreign Office. Brian wrote to an old friend, Alec Randall. Randall, however, had moved on and the new mandarins were frosty in their notes to each other. "I suggest that we should, in reply, tell Lt-Col Giffey that his brother-in-law should make application for a visa in Stockholm in the usual way, and let the refusal be given by the PCO [Passport Control Officer] there in due course. We cannot discuss this question with Lt-Col Giffey."[18] Brian accordingly received a standard reply, telling him that London was not the right place to apply for a visa if the person in question was living in Stockholm.

By that time Brian had found new employment, something that Anni had been praying for: "He's a born worker and time lies heavily on his hands, and he frets," she said. "We were saved, it seemed as by a miracle," was Brian's reaction. He was going to be "re-embodied and employed on the Control Commission staff for Germany," as his regimental records put it. This meant that, having retired twice from the Worcestershire Regiment, Brian had now re-joined it. Anni believed this made him very happy because he had been made a lieutenant-colonel.[19] "I should be proud of it that Brian, being 57, is still going to be put into uniform and that he can serve his country." She was less certain about her own changed position. "I have no idea how I will like life being a soldier's wife. We are used to being free, but a soldier is a soldier and even if I'm not in uniform I'm also a soldier, Brian says," Anni told her mother in Sweden.[20] Now that her family were safely out of occupied Estonia, Anni wrote to them often.

The war was not yet over but London, looking ahead, perceived a need for a system to establish law and order in post-war Germany. The Allies had set up the Control Commission for Germany. In September 1944 there was already an urgency in Britain about hiring staff. The Public Safety Branch, Brian's new employer, explained the rush of his recruitment as follows: "Such was the urgency of the provision of the necessary staff for the Control Commission at that time, that, on receiving your verbal assurance that the recall of this officer to the Active List was a formality in view of his special qualifications and medical fitness, he was instructed to report for duty with effect from 25 Sep and has continued to work with this Branch ever since."[21]

Brian's first assignment was to attend a five-week course at Southlands College in Wimbledon. After three months of inactivity Brian enjoyed it enormously. There were lectures on refugees, office management and technical facilities. "I'm having the time of my life," he told Anni, "am very busy indeed, and likely to be busier still. It's all frightfully interesting and a most pleasant crowd, excellent place." The Giffeys continued to stay with the Jakobsons in Surrey and Brian came home to Anni at week-ends, but he was rearing to go to Berlin. "There is nothing on earth I want so much as to help in this great work on the Commission, where we are supposed to go – and that

I should return to soldiering would be the final satisfaction." He was full of admiration for Winston Churchill whose prefabricated harbours for the Normandy landings had been a secret up until recently. Altogether the prime minister seemed to Brian a "grand fellow" whose treatment of Hitler reminded him "of Homeric heroes slanging their opponents."

When Brian finally left for Germany in July 1945, Anni stayed behind. She was not at all happy about that, but had to wait until the conditions improved so that all wives could be brought over. Brian didn't like the thought of leaving her either. He was particularly concerned that she would be on her own, so he invented a compromise. Anni was to move in with Claire at Lenham. Undercliffe was a substantial house, big enough for the two women and Claire's recently adopted son, David (who for some reason was called John). The initial plan was that Anni would help Claire to look after the child. David was eight and Claire, who had not remarried, was 60.

Anni agreed to the plan; she always wanted to please her husband. However, it soon became clear that house share with Claire was very difficult. Anni found Claire's ways too different from her own. Claire got up early in the morning and wanted Anni to do the same, but Anni liked to sleep late and took exception to the noise Claire made to wake her. Claire also invited confidences without offering anything in return; Anni disliked that. She found Claire intrusive, mean and calculating. Even Claire's stepson became a bone of contention. David was at home for summer holidays (he attended boarding school) but was told to do homework seven days a week, leaving hardly any time for play. Claire also shouted at him, kept reminding him that he was only an adopted child and deprived him of sugar and other foods. Anni remonstrated and complained to Brian. She also asked a London friend to find her a flat so that she could leave Undercliffe. Anni's diary has survived but it is frankly uninteresting: she either misses Brian, disagrees with Claire or adores Claire's new puppy, Doe.

Brian wrote daily from Germany, sounding very patient. "But go on, bring your troubles to Daddy, as before, my Poppet. Lean on Bron, my Bryn, lean on the shoulder of the strong hill, fair little hill, nestle close up to the side of the big hill that God gave strength to shelter you." As to Claire, Brian said that "she is the only person in the world, apart from you my Dearest, who in the least belongs to me, and the only one of my friends of my youth – middle manhood – (almost the only person alive with whom I share the experiences and memories of my first 47 years) – who is not dead or God knows where – surely, you, to whom your family means so much, must understand! I want to keep in touch with her." Brian's mother had died in 1936 and he had no family whatsoever left. "I cannot cease to love her as a friend," he said of Claire, acutely aware of a need for atonement: "What I did to Claire was terrible and might have had so very different an effect on her. Yet she never ceased to be my staunch and loyal friend," he insisted.

Meanwhile Ants Oras managed to obtain a six-months British visa (Sandy McKibbin may have helped) and his arrival from Stockholm eased Anni's situation at Undercliffe. Brother and sister had a lot of catching up to do – they had not seen each other for five years. Once Ants

46. Ants Oras, Anni's brother.

left for Norwich to work in a library, Anni moved out as well. Installed at Kendrick Place in London, she felt free after four long months with Claire. Lenham had never felt like home and Anni felt shy of Claire who was "a fussy old woman".

Meanwhile Brian was representing a victorious occupying power in post-war Germany. This meant that he was well provided for, while witnessing the daily struggles the Berliners experienced. The city was in a terrible state. "Here in Berlin the winter will be hard – very little food for the Germans, less coal and shelter. The town is in ruins, and to get even the most primitive accommodation for the majority of the 3 ¾ millions will take much time," Brian told his wife. He travelled around and saw the contrasts. The whole country was broken. "By road and rail, I've run through the peaceful countryside – and small towns – for half an hour or more at a stretch and never seen a sign of a bomb. Then suddenly: a big factory completely destroyed; a railway bridge: just twisted iron surrounded by bomb-craters; a railway crossing or junction and adjoining crossroads: a close pattern of craters and general destruction. Hamm Marshalling Yard is enormous; though we bombed it for five years on end the Germans never seem to have by-passed it, to have provided alternatives – typical of these very inelastic people. Bielefeld is the greatest scene of destruction I've seen, Bielefeld and Dortmund – much worse than Berlin. In the midst of it all the ruined tower of a ruined church, with the bells rolling out their deep toned message."[22]

Working in the Internal Affairs and Communications Division of the Public Safety Branch in Berlin, Brian was not short of anything. "We live pleasantly, indeed I feel ashamed that I live so well, happy, – as far as I can be happy without you," he told Anni. The Americans provided particularly good lunches and one day "we had what at home would be 10 days meat ration in the form of one e-nor-mous succulent grilled steak, fat as a fist and all rosy inside, with fried onions and asparagus-tips salad."

Brian developed the habit of keeping a few "nice things" in his office for emergencies. One day, he told Anni, he saw a clean but poor woman with two small children near his office, brought them in, told them to wait and went upstairs to fetch the chocolate he had in reserve in a drawer. In his room, however, he found that a cup of tea and a bun had been delivered for his elevenses. "So I took the bun as well as the chocolate, and it was terribly pathetic to see how the little kiddies' eyes shone when they saw the bun, just the bun, as I was coming down the steps to them. I don't think they had realised about the chocolate yet. I couldn't spare much else just then, but had a full box of matches for the mother – matches are 1/6 d (3 Marks) on the black market."

Another moving story concerned his Jewish art teacher. Brian, an enthusiastic amateur, had joined an art class. The old man who led the class had had a hard time under Hitler, was arrested and released three times, and had survived thanks to his wife's Aryan family. It was late autumn when Brian told Anni that "he and his wife now have just got glass in their windows, and coal but – though 'victims of fascism' [they] have so far been unable to get a stove." One day the teacher dropped a worn glove in the underground, bent down to retrieve it and found it was gone. Brian, who felt that he had learnt more from him than from any other art teacher, went out and bought him a new warm pair – not difficult for him as an officer. Writing to Anni, he was looking forward to the moment of handover, to seeing the old man smile with pleasure.

Alongside these individual stories, Brian knew there were much bigger issues at stake. It was important, he said, that

Anni should understand the work he and others were doing. Germany had been militarised and nazified, but henceforth needed to function as a civil society. This was the task of the Public Safety Branch, with a particular emphasis on the police and fire services. "You see, we've come to stay," he told her. "We've taken over the government of these people, and thus we have assumed responsibility for them. We must, we will, and we do give them good government, the best kind we know, government on the British model. That, at the same time, is the best way as we see it of re-educating Germany."

Brian followed the same principles as chairman of the mess committee, in which capacity he had a number of local staff to manage. With time they came to trust him with their tales of husbands or sons lost in the war. Brian seized on this opportunity to "govern and re-educate" these German women.

Chapter 10

Denazification in post-war Germany

From September 1945 Brian represented Britain on the Nazi Arrest and Denazification (NAD) Sub-Committee at its meetings in the splendid Allied Control Authority building in Berlin. The same way as Germany was divided into four zones, the four Allies – Britain, the USA, France and the Soviet Union – each provided a member for the sub-committee, plus there were observers, secretaries and interpreters, close to 20 people in total. Each member was expected to make short and concise statements and these were translated by official interpreters without interruptions, but the system didn't always work. "When the interpreters break down, as happened again five times in Russian and twice in French – not because they lack knowledge of the languages concerned, but lack grasp, background – and interest, I take over the translation and all understand and are fully in the picture," Brian noted with self-satisfaction. He thrived in the months Britain, i.e. Lt-Col Giffey, was in the chair.

Interpreting was simple, Brian argued. All one needed was three components: comprehensive knowledge, precision of mind and imagination. "Handling my Sub-Committee gives me interest and sense of power," he told Anni. He got on well with the others on the sub-committee, but realised that they were "working to different instructions, on different lines, with such different backgrounds and, my word! yes! excepting me who thinks in all their languages, all, even the interpreters (excepting one who thinks in two) thinking in different languages."

The sub-committee reported to the Public Safety Committee, chaired by Frederick Isemonger, with whom Brian shared billets in the pleasant suburb of Grünewald.[1] Brian called him Old Eye or simply E. "He's charming, considerate, most fair and himself most active and energetic ('do it now'), but much senior and it is good for me to have to do the job for someone like that after being Chief for so many years and then pretty level with most I worked with," Brian told Anni. "We share many a joke and many a more serious experience, both at work and outside, and it has been a delight to me." Isemonger had a police background: he had been the inspector-general of Indian police in the Northwest Frontier Province.

At week-ends Brian and Isemonger went sailing on Lake Havel. "Indeed I am lucky to have a boss, with a car of his own, who is as keen on sailing and on ships as I." Brian was also pleased to be trusted: "My boss leaves more and more Staff work, and even Police work, to me, and while he is on leave I'm to do detailed reconnaissance and report on another of our Metropolitan 'Divisions'."

The subject of denazification was huge and complex; it affected every walk of life from schools and banks to transport. In the initial stages the sub-committee laid down general principles. Each member reported on the progress made in his zone; together they were to draft an agreed and uniform policy on the arrest of Nazis and their removal from public office.[2] A month later a draft was complete and Brian rejoiced: "Yesterday my Sub-committee at last finished its Magnum Opus for good and we got agreement on it at last – on the 54th day... I have certainly been very lucky over the whole thing and received support from my own crowd and others and friendliness from everybody. There has been a wonderful sort of camaraderie about the whole Sub-committee, which has really warmed my heart."

The 9 November meeting, however, was "momentous", Brian said. "It was the 16th, and at it we reached complete agreement on the other of the two Directives which, both, we were charged to prepare on Aug 30th. On the first, as you know already, we reached complete agreement somewhere between Oct 20th, Oct 24th. This one we had sent off earlier, with plenty of dissentient views and a sharp conflict of principle with the Americans; any 'agreed version' appeared out of the question. Our symposium of contradictions was returned to us with the instruction 'to think again and to think alike' or, at any rate, to produce a single, agreed text." As the meeting progressed, just "one last point of essential difference remained between the Americans and us and might well wreck the whole show," Brian said.

Never shy about his own achievements, he added dramatically: "Suddenly the moment had arrived. And impromptu, at dictation speed I dictated the text which, I thought, I could concede and which 'would let them [Americans] out'. They accepted and it was all over. The greater part of the centre final text, of this Directive as of the other, is mine, and I've already had a bouquet from the Brigadier."[3] The Brigadier was George Heyman, deputy chief of the HQ Branch of the Internal Affairs and Communications Division. A day later Brian concluded with satisfaction: "I've never worked harder than this week. Some of the work has been really important, and this morning my Brigadier said that a difficult letter I had dictated 'expressed exactly what he had in mind'."[4]

Brian's daily letters to Anni ran to several pages, sometimes with drawings in the margins to amuse her. "You see, I must tell you of everything that happens to me; of my work I tell you little because much is confidential," he wrote. On another day he got carried away, describing the painfully slow discussions at great length, only then to stop to wonder: "Sweetheart, are you interested, or does it bore you stiff? I do feel that telling you everything about everything and everybody – just as you do – brings and keeps us near to each other."[5]

47. Brian's drawing of the slow progress of quadripartite talks.

Anni meanwhile was sending daily letters from London. She had no committee work to describe, nothing but her domestic chores. One might wonder what effect such letters had on Brian. The two lovers, however, had a desperate need to encourage and support each other, despite the physical distances between them and the vagaries of the postal system. Brian was always bitterly disappointed when the daily letter from Anni failed to materialise and grew anxious when a second day passed without. Usually the missing envelopes turned up together with a couple of days' delay.

"Darling, I just can't describe to you how I love and enjoy your letters," Brian enthused. "For me there isn't a dull page or sentence in them. The way your deepest thoughts and deepest feelings, and your wise and kind ideas about people, get mixed up with the books you read and the food you prepare and eat, the undies you make for yourself (and the great adventure of the heavy skirt you altered), the walks you do and the shopping, the people you meet and pass the time of day with, the work, the washing, the cleaning and polishing of the room, the weather – all, all you share with me, I live with you and feel and enjoy with absorbed interest, tenderness and enjoyment. For me your letters are perfect. That, I suppose is why we fell in love so utterly – because we suit and understand and fit each other and each other's ideas so perfectly." There is no doubt about the sincerity of Brian's admiration. He thought Anni's letters were lovely, reflecting "true poetry of love and longing".

Apart from the meetings, there were also amusing incidents that Brian described for Anni's entertainment. He travelled a fair amount and wrote about things he saw; at times incompetence and mismanagement arrived at his doorstep. Enthusiastic men in heavy boots nearly removed all the furniture from their billet and it was a matter of luck that Isemonger was around to stop that nonsense. In January Brian's car broke down ten miles into the Russian zone, he and a colleague faced the prospect of spending a night in a cold car in what amounted to alien territory. Brian turned this chilling incident into a jolly yarn, describing how he and the other man sweated, pushing the vehicle all the way back to Helmstedt, the zonal border town where they were able to stay overnight in the British zone.

Another transport story concerned the French on his sub-committee, who were chronically late for meetings, having 18 miles to cover in poor transport. Brian observed that the French had built up a reputation and "whenever they're late, they're met with ready sympathy instead of black looks; everybody assumes that they've been unlucky again; we commiserate before they have time to explain. I can imagine a Frenchman, disinclined to get up, stretching, murmuring: 'I think I shall have had a puncture this morning', and going to sleep for another half-hour," Brian chuckled.

His linguistic skills were called for when some Russians unexpectedly arrived at the Transport Division and no interpreter was available. Why had the visitors come, a British lieutenant-colonel wanted to know. He had already set up an appointment for 2.30 with a Russian major; they had agreed to meet at the docks to examine barge owners and skippers to determine that all barges had been duly registered. And yet three visitors arrived at midday: a Russian colonel, a captain and a third man, all scowling. One of the Russians told Brian that they had been detailed in place of the major, so Brian assumed that that was the problem. He asked the men to confirm that they would be at the docks at 2.30 and the matter would be settled. Only then it turned out that the Russians had something else in mind.

"Couldn't we go right now?" they wanted to know.

What followed amounted to a chat about lunching arrangements.

"I see, 2.30 is too near your dinner hour, which is at 3," Brian said. "But ours is at 1, and if he goes now the unfortunate colonel will get nothing at all to eat."

"Couldn't the colonel send a junior officer?" the Russians enquired.

"His dinner hour is also at 1, and he would go hungry. Could you not make it tomorrow morning, say 10, or 11 or 11.30?"

A brief consultation followed, then the Russians shook their heads. "No, we have conferences; couldn't do a morning before Saturday." By Saturday, however, the British colonel would be in Antwerp, so that would not work either. Further discussion enabled Brian to fix the visit for 12.30 on the following day, the colonel having said that he'd make special arrangements for lunch. This left Brian to conclude: "Lucky I really know Russian well, as the [Russian] colonel had an impediment in his speech. Also that I know German; the third man turned out to be a German, who knew Russian but no English, and knew the meeting-place, which the Russians didn't."

Brian admired the Russians he had seen at Helmstedt, the Russian border post: "The Russians salute very smartly – they were a good deal in evidence near the border – and their officers are resplendent with shoulder pieces [badges of rank] of a size and splendour unknown in the West." However, the Russian HQ at Karlshorst, about 18 miles from the British zone, was "so inaccessible that even on a week-day, when our visit was announced and all prepared, and we did get through the barriers after having been kept waiting and put off with the silliest tripe for hours – got through eventually by i) good luck, ii) my swearing vigorously in Russian, iii) the favour of the Gods." One of Brian's favourite Russian expressions was "the devil take it"; it was in frequent use. He got on well with Americans and was amused to quote what "Old Robertson, the Tennesseean and US Secretary of the Public Safety Committee," had said after they had visited the Russian HQ: "I was awfully glad to have you with me, I mean you being able to speak to them in their own language. I've been to see them four times before, but I've only got through once, and then it took me much longer – about three hours!"

In his letters to Anni Brian made hardly any unkind comments about the Russians; he called Lt-Col Sychev on the NAD sub-committee "my friend". However, Brian's views can't have been much different from those of his SIS colleague, Frank Foley, who said that "Russia is a cruel and bloody country, at least their government is. I had quite a lot to do with high-ranking Russian officers in Berlin and liked them but they were terrified of their own government. I am sick and tired of those tyrannical dictators. Without them Europe would settle down easily."[6]

48. Allied Control Authority building (Kammergericht) where quadripartite meetings were held.

Brian and Foley worked closely together in Berlin although Brian was no longer with SIS and Foley was the SIS representative in the Public Safety Branch, with the official title of assistant inspector-general.[7] At times they attended committee meetings together. When Brian was on leave Foley stood in for him. Sometimes intelligence matters came up at meetings, since many areas were of interest to intelligence. Archives, for example. Brian, on behalf of the British government, objected to the plan to move the Nazi Party archives from Munich to Berlin. Counter-intelligence occasionally came up. Chairing a meeting, Brian said that "the primary responsibility for arrest and/or investigation belonged to Counter Intelligence, a military organisation, but that British Public Safety officers and the German police, acting under their orders were used on occasion to assist Counter Intelligence in this matter."[8]

Foley was a passport control officer in pre-war Berlin. He saved 10,000 Jews, his biography says. It is, however, likely that many passport control officers saved people, and not only Jews. Anni has recalled how, after her appendix operation in June 1940, a man came to see Brian, who was the passport control officer in Tallinn. "I was still convalescing at home when Leo came to see you – it is not his real name – we gave to so many people nicknames that often the real names are forgotten, and it is better so – he had to get out of Estonia and needed your help. I remember he brought me the biggest bouquet of dark red roses I've ever had – he was nice. You and someone else did help him to get out. We met him again years later in Tel Aviv and in Baghdad. He stayed with us several times." There were few Jews in pre-war Estonia but there may have been other, no less deserving cases, whom Brian helped in Tallinn.

Brian was happy to help post-war Estonian refugees whenever he could and gently chided Anni on this subject: "I grieve that you should be still a little shy of asking my help for your people. Perhaps it is good that you should feel like that...

But I want you to understand... I welcome the chance and am glad and proud of it and happy to be able to help a little when it is so much needed." He wanted to make sure that Anni had heard him: "And will you, at once, Miss! do you hear? stop being sensitive and feeling bad when I make use of my right of re-paying a little of that great debt of happiness and love and loyalty that I owe the Orases and above all, to you." Some relatives of Anni wrote to her for help and it is likely that Brian was able to assist.

January 1946 brought particular joy because the draft Brian had worked on passed into law. He told Anni: "Incidentally, I and – and those who worked with me have had the immense satisfaction to see our 'Nazi Removal and Exclusion Directive', the one on which we worked for 56 days, beginning on Aug 31st, and eventually reached agreement – the first (I have been told) on which quadripartite agreement was ever reached, become Military Government Law by quadripartite acceptance on the highest level and quadripartite signature on Jan 12 – without any material alteration – about 20 foolscap pages of closely typed text."

An important milestone, this still left plenty to do. For example, much work went into the documentation and clearance of foreign barge crews navigating on inland waterways in Germany, and of German crews in neighbouring countries. At one meeting "we spent one entire day on one foolscap page," Brian complained. "Everybody fought everything, and everybody else's amendments." Nobody seemed to be in good form and Brian was held back by a signal he had received from his superiors in London (the Foreign Office) that made it impossible for him to discuss an entire class of individuals, so he had to keep quiet. Also, he heard that his "friend Sychov" had had a nervous breakdown.

The paper on the arrest, trial and punishment of the war criminals, Nazis and militarists and the internments, control and surveillance of the potentially dangerous Germans was "frightfully involved", Brian said. He had drafted parts of it, Foley had honed it further, but once the London authorities sent their comments it fell to Brian to check that the versions agreed. "The amount of work involved in checking and comparing the two, or rather three, was thus terrific. With all the interruptions of telephone calls, consultations and other piecemeal work at the office, I did not get very far, and took the work home with me." He sat up until 3.30 am, satisfied with what he had done, but apologetic, too, because of the lateness of the hour. He had promised to Anni to look after himself.

At one point there were meetings every other day and Brian found this very tiring. "Well, I'd worked rather late last night, preparing the draft for the British-French-US-Russian Agreement on Interzonal Travel, – all that, as you already know, after a very full day of running, sailing, painting and an evening in the Mess with a certain amount of Mess business. I walked home through a velvet night about 12.15; got out of my clothes and settled down to work."

Language, and Russian in particular, fascinated Brian. "It's the Russian month (Chairmanship of the Committees and Duty Secretaries). And I found that they had translated our General Report of Denazification in the British Zone and Sector of Berlin terribly badly. No ill will, just didn't grasp the meaning of the English text in a large number of cases." So Brian translated the whole thing, about a page, and submitted it to the Russians with a polite little note to say that it did not pretend to be a good translation but he simply wanted to render the correct meaning. "And would you believe it!" he told Anni with glee, "they corrected two of my spelling mistakes... and for the rest printed my translation into Russian word for word, and it has now become the official Soviet text! I do consider this to be a feather in my cap and am really quite proud. I certainly had no hopes of this when I first heard Russian spoken at the age of 30, and sat down to learn it at the age of 40!"

Brian got on well with everybody, but he liked the Americans in particular. For one thing, they laid on excellent food. An inspection of recently discovered International CID records included lunch and Brian went along. "The Americans had included me in the invitation – they're always awfully nice to me, because (I think) I know so much about the American Civil War. And Old E. had accepted for me, because 1) he thought the records would be interesting and instructive, 2) he knew the lunch would be super and 3) because I'd keep the Russians and the French amused. As a matter of fact the records were disappointing," Brian said, having thoroughly enjoyed the outing.

He was also invited to an American wedding – pure Hollywood, he concluded, having witnessed the newlyweds' prolonged kiss at the altar. The church, St Anne's in Dahlem, was small but exquisite, he observed. The service, in English, conducted by the well-known pastor Martin Niemöller, was in Brian's opinion marred by the fact that the pastor spoke at length about his incarceration at Sachsenhausen and Dachau concentration camps where he had spent eight long years. Brian had an opportunity to talk to him later and concluded that the man was essentially a Prussian naval officer. "In his conversation with me at the reception it became quite clear that the cause which he felt to have been his was, largely at least, that of the Wehrmacht (as well as the Protestant Church) against the Nazis rather than that of Humanity, and Democracy, against aggressive militarism," he told Anni.[9]

Brian began to consider joining the Special Police Corps, the Blue Caps, as they were called, once the War Office began cutting staff. The plan was to limit the number of officers within the entire Control Commission to 500. Very much aware of his age, Brian told Anni: "I am not going back on my decision to strain every nerve and, if necessary, risk rebuffs in my determination to do all I can to get and keep work, to earn money for you, and for you and the others. But unless I can get fairly decent terms in this bleeding Blue Corps outfit – a long contract and some chance of promotion – it will be a sorry business. There will be no permanence or security or authority about it."[10] Fellow officers suggested that joining the corps would amount to demotion. On the other hand, the rumour had it that he might be made redundant after Christmas 1946, and so the die was cast. Financially it would not be bad, he reckoned. "That would give us £500: £100 for Bee and £400 for us and the family."[11] Bee was Brian's ex-wife Claire to whom he was paying £10 in maintenance every month and the family were Anni's mother and sisters, refugees in Sweden.

When, in 1947, Brian joined the Special Police Corps, he was required to attend a refresher course at the Control Office Depot and Training Centre, better known as Bletchley Park. At first it seemed ridiculous to be sent all that way to listen to lectures on things he already knew. He told Anni: "Here please hold your sides to prevent your splitting them with laughing – I've got to go to Bletchley for a week's course to learn all about Germany and how to work as a member of the Control Commission for Germany (British Element) – PS Branch and all that, and what conditions are like!!!" Once at Bletchley, however, he changed his mind. One of the talks he enjoyed was "a very good and interesting review of the circumstances that led up to the planning for the post-war occupation and control of the Axis Power (began in 1942!) – by Civil Affairs under the War Office, Control Commission under the Foreign Office and, after Moscow, by the 'European Advisory Committee' of the 'Big Three'. It at all events cleared my mind on the way the whole thing hung together."

Lectures on German history were particularly enjoyable. "I would gladly pay £1 to be able to take you to hear all three and hear them again with you," Brian told Anni. Major Horn invited Brian to do some lecturing and he jumped at the opportunity. Even talks on the Allied Control Authority did not dim his enthusiasm. "Here I was on familiar ground, but none the less learnt much, as: about the relations of the British Element with HM Government as regards policy, and how the Council of Foreign Ministers comes into the picture. The film: 'Defeated Nation' [was about] conditions in the British Zone. Excellent propaganda for reconstruction of a healthy German economic, and general life. The spoken propaganda on practical, commonsense, selfish grounds. The human appeal is unspoken – it is made by the pictures."

At Bletchley the men were vaccinated against typhus and tuberculosis and inoculated with the typhoid and paratyphoid vaccine. They were now military public safety officers, civilian members of the Special Police Corps. In the post-war rationing climate they were given a "uniform grant (£50) and clothing coupons (240)"; and "If the complete uniform is not ready by the time an officer leaves for Germany, he may travel in khaki battle-dress with Police markings, and blue cap. Khaki battle-dress, webbing equipment, revolver and greatcoat are issued, on loan and free of charge, at Bletchley."[12]

Anni, too, needed inoculations because, at long last, she was about to join her husband in Berlin. Ironically, however, Brian was still at Bletchley, worried that Anni might have to travel while he was in England, but eventually things worked out just fine. Anni survived the crossing of the Channel, held on to the taffrail (as Brian had instructed) and attached the right colour labels (blue and orange) to herself and her luggage (as Brian had reminded her more than once).

They had been apart for 20 months, their longest separation. Once reunited, their daily letters stopped. It is known that theirs was a small flat with a beautiful parquet floor and balcony where Anni grew flowers and vegetables from seed. Sailing took up many a week-end and the British Club's excellent orchestra allowed the couple to dance to their old favourites (the tangoes Violetta and Comparsita in particular).

A visit to Hamburg proved that the city was in a healthier state than Berlin. "We were very much struck by the appearance of the Germans in Hamburg (and indeed of the town) as compared with Berlin. In Hamburg the people looked healthy, cheerful and very much alive. There is a tremendous amount of traffic. Children sing, and there is much animated conversation and laughter. Bomb damage is little in evidence, as ruined buildings have been cleared away and more lightly damaged buildings have been repaired. Nowhere is the difference between the British Zone and Berlin more marked than in Hamburg."[13] These positive comments sound remarkable. Just four years had passed since the 1943 bombing that left Hamburg badly fire-damaged.

Alarming changes were taking place in Berlin where the Soviets cut land access and airlifts had to be organised to provide the population with basic goods. Changes occurred elsewhere in Europe and Brian was concerned about the extent of Soviet bullying. "Stalin himself of course – just like Hitler – would prefer conquest without war by infiltration, disruption and sudden seizure or gradual absorption of one country after another rather than by fighting, but he has almost reached the end of what he can accomplish without open hostility and he is stepping on the gas because he fears the effect of the Marshall plan. It is becoming clear to the most average intelligence that we must call a halt, must resist by every effective means if one country after another, and finally Great Britain, is not to become a Czecho-Slovakia."[14]

Brian hoped that the Soviet takeover of Czechoslovakia would jolt the complacent West and save the Finns. "I agree that none but people with criminal mentality want a third world war. Certainly no nation wants it, but unfortunately the Russian people and the vassals of the Soviet power are not asked. And the Russians are being exclusively fed on propaganda and 'misinformation' for so many years that young and middle-aged people nowadays have never known anything else. Their leaders have planned world conquest by armed force or the threat of armed force since 1928 [when the Comintern programme was adopted at its 6th congress], and never wavered in their aim. Anyone who is acquainted with Stalin's speeches even in recent years knows that."[15]

Anni's brother Ants Oras published the *Baltic Eclipse* in London in 1948. The book was a personal take on recent political events in Estonia. Brian found it excellent and told Ants: "I devoured [it] in the two nights following its arrival, reading it until 3 am and 2 am respectively. Anni and I knew that it would be an important book, that it would be well written, that it would be a masterly account of the facts, and a valuable historical document and a powerful and convincing indictment of the oppressors of Estonia and the enemies of freedom, and that it would do all that Estonians themselves and friends of Estonia and her people would expect you to give. But my dear Ants, we didn't know that you could write like that. That you had such authorship, such gift of divine fire." Brian praised Ants for his understatement: "Your burning indignation and grief at the suffering of your unhappy people must have made such restraint – a restraint comparable to that of Pericles' funeral oration – a matter of severest self-discipline... Previously I had only read your work on Milton; I had considered you 'academic'. I did not know that you had so warm, easy and natural humanity or that you could express it on paper."[16]

Ants did altogether well in 1948: he was at last offered a professorship of English literature at the University of Florida. The news, however, made Brian promptly issue a strong warning to him. Was he fully aware of Soviet bullying tactics, he wondered. If the SS Stefan Batory Ants and his wife Liivi intended to take belonged to a Polish company based in Britain there was nothing to worry about, but Brian urged caution if the owner was "the Soviet Vassal Polish Government". "Anni and I are very alarmed at the latter possibility, because the Polish Government and its agencies are anything but free, and for their Soviet masters it might be highly desirable that the author of 'Baltic Eclipse' should not reach the wider sphere of activity which the USA offer, and still more attractive to get him into their power. Both in Berlin and in the Border areas of the British Zone we are only too well acquainted with Russian kidnapping habits," Brian said, outlining a few basic precautions for Ants to follow.[17]

Ants took Brian's warning seriously and wrote to his future boss in Gainsville, Florida, just in case. "The 'Batory' is government-owned," he admitted, "and I have no doubt whatever that it will be swarming with Soviet agents, but then so is probably every other liner crossing the Atlantic in either direction... In case we do not arrive, – a most unlikely assumption – enquiries should naturally be made. My brother-in-law – not an alarmist – definitely advises me to make sure that some American of standing as well as an Estonian knowing the communist 'tricks' should meet us in New York."[18]

Estonian KGB files show that Brian's worries for Ants's safety were not without foundation. The KGB described Ants as a "well-known" American agent whose anti-Soviet and defamatory book had been commissioned by his masters.[19]

By the time Ants and Liivi made their Atlantic crossing – uneventfully, it needs to be said – Brian was transferred to Bünde in Germany where he became the liaison officer for Mr. M.S. O'Rorke, the public safety adviser. O'Rorke had first approached Brian, suggesting liaison with the Legal Division. "He asked me how I liked the idea," Brian chuckled. "I said 'I like it fine', but was 'only a bogus policeman and no lawyer at all'. He said 'oh that doesn't matter at all, you have a tidy mind'." In Berlin Brian had often been asked to vet Germans for the Legal Division as a matter of urgency and this may have commended him to O'Rorke.

Brian had only good words to say about his new position in Bünde: "It's a most attractive job, but an absorbing one and I have been very worried whether I shall be able to keep anywhere near abreast with it. Apart from the liaison with Legal, requiring about 3 visits a week – there are heaps of Committee Meetings, Working Parties and Conferences to attend and Staff Studies and drafts to be written and cases to be worked up. It would be enough to keep two men busy, there is besides the hackwork of constant enquiries coming in, countless communications to be sent out, and everything about which there is a legal touch or something approaching a legal character used to come to JD [Brian's predecessor] and is likely to come to me."[20]

Bünde was a "nice sleepy little country town", at its best in spring. Later in the year Brian concluded that "here we have had seven wonderful months; I don't think I have been as perfectly happy even in a Mess of my own regiment as with these charming Policemen at the Public Safety Adviser's Office, some of whom I knew in England four years ago, and most of them in Berlin during the two years and nine months I was there, who have made me so entirely one of themselves."

However, Brian was worried, perhaps unduly so, about his ability to keep in work. This was not a new worry either. In September 1946 he had already feared that once he and Anni returned to Britain they would be impoverished. "Life will be drab and monotonous," he told her. "We shall not be able to afford to buy this, or do that. You will miss all the little comforts – and the respect and consideration – the privacy you have been accustomed to and come to regard as your right. It will be hard enough for me to see you 'do without'. Be patient with me when the time comes."

A year later Brian felt confident that they had survived the danger of redundancy for another twelve months. Alas, in the autumn of 1948 Brian wrote: "Here my contract is finished and I should have left on Aug 31st. With the progressive reduction in our strength and at my age, the IG [inspector general] could not get it renewed. For a year and more I have been one of only two non-policemen left, we are down to half our original establishment and in a year's time may be down to one-sixth. At present the IG is hanging on to me from week to week (I am safe until Dec 31st and then shall get a month's pay at home while looking for a job) and has done everything he could to get me another job out here, but everybody is cutting down, all good men are 'sponsored' and when a man is well over sixty it means one competitor the less."

And so it was no surprise that Brian was made redundant in early 1949. The Giffeys returned to London, once again homeless and jobless. Brian was a few months short of 62. This did not prevent him from feeling that he could still be useful. He told Anni: "You see, I should be in the War against those bloody Soviet Bastards more than ever, be helping poor and deserving Allies, could no doubt help them more than anyone else in a dozen ways, and liaising for them with our own people."[21]

Having made him redundant, the Foreign Office put him in touch with the Association of Ukrainians in Great Britain, which needed an English correspondent. Brian liked the idea immediately. "I shall be doing a man's work, and feel a man again," he said, pleased to be able to help people who needed help and his skills in Russian. The pay was not great but it doubled their current income. As liaison officer he would be in touch with the Home Office and read more Russian than English and thus keep alive "the biggest asset I've got," he told Anni, who was holidaying in Teignmouth.[22]

Brian threw himself into his new job. "Work? I'll love it; it's really worth while," he said in July 1949. "Welfare for 40,000 in Great Britain, and carrying on the Cold War. And the people here, mostly very simple, are really nice. Thank God this job gives me a chance to help and to be of real use, and even smooth over difficulties." The job was practically tailor-made, he said. "It's as if the Gods said: 'All your life might have trained you for this. The four years with the Police have taught you quick decision, and to write snappily and convincingly on anything. Soon you will start meeting people, and to speak convincingly. More than ever you have a chance to help poor people, to relieve suffering, to bring gladness into drab lives, and to smooth over the troubles of those whom misunderstanding has put at loggerheads. The people you work with are nice people, and wholly admirable in many ways. And you are helping, and preparing the fight against the enemies of God, and man, and Liberty – human health and happiness. If your pay is no more than will keep you going it will give you the distinction of being disinterested. We have brought you through life in comfort and ease. The future is on the knees of Zeus as yet, our father. Go to it and serve our purpose well. Again we have found you a happy home: indeed two homes. Always you have been able to spend freely. If now you have to economise and spend sparingly it will be useful discipline, and it will make you more at one with those you work for and with, from whom material ease might have set you apart."[23]

The work continued to involve him and he admitted, when writing to a friend, that he had done nothing to find a better-paid job. "I work really terribly hard – apart from working long hours at the office, give German lessons to a couple two evenings a week and now teach a Hungarian Jewess English."

In 1953 the Giffeys at last found a permanent home at 78 Southwold Mansions, Widley Road. They rented two very nice rooms and a tiny one, a lovely kitchen and lovely bathroom, Brian said. Light and sunny, two and a half floors up (with landing) – a dream come true. The couple had not had a holiday for three years. "We're both half worked to death, and all we want is to lie on our backs, in an orchard or on a cliff, and look at the sky, and not to have to prepare a single meal or wash up. I work 60 hours a week and Anni little less, and we hardly ever relax," Brian told a friend.[24] Why and how they had exhausted themselves to this degree is not explained, but Brian taught more and more evening classes and possibly tired himself out by travelling from one venue to another. He

49. The Giffeys in the 1950s.

continued to work for the Ukrainians until 1958, but even after retirement he still taught an evening class. Physically weaker, his drive was undiminished.

He had a hernia operation at St Mary's Hospital in August 1960. Two weeks later he was invited to teach a class on life and institutions for a year and he accepted. A friend said: "What a chap Giffey is, had operation 11 days ago and has bullied doctors into letting him out to be ready in time for start of term." A hip operation followed in 1963.

Brian Giffey died on 28 December 1967 at the age of 80. After his death Anni continued to live at 78 Southwold Mansions until she died on 2 February 2000. She was 88, still slim as a teenager. Although the couple had discussed adoption, they died childless.

Chapter 11

Afterthoughts

Anni Giffey has claimed a much bigger part of Brian's biography than I originally intended. Initially I may not have fully appreciated her role, but most of Brian's letters were addressed to her, much information about Brian has come from her. She was a native of Estonia where Brian was assigned on his first intelligence job, and he left the country only because its independence was stolen by the Soviets in 1940. That was the year when Anni was separated from her beloved family, forced to leave because she had become a British subject (while proud to be Mrs C.K.O.B. Giffey). Afterwards she often thought, with concern, of her country and people. It was only after the war, in 1947, that she was able to visit her mother and sisters, who by then had become refugees in Sweden. They had fled Estonia because they didn't want to live in the Soviet Union. After 1991 when Estonia's independence was restored, Anni no longer had reason to return to her homeland: she had no family there and she was 80 years old.

Immediately after her husband's death in 1967 Anni kept a diary, as if still writing to him. She found it impossible to complete Brian's memoirs, and this worried her. "Again and again you told me if you should die before me I should finish the 'Job in Hand' for you, but my darling – I cannot. There are such awful gaps – how can I write about your Russian campaign? I do not even know how long you were there. I know you have told me this and that, some of it I vaguely remember but, as you know, I've never been a good listener and so much of it has gone."[1]

She read and reread Brian's versions of the "Job in Hand". "There are at least 6-7 beginnings," she concluded, "more or less the same. Lots about your forebears, lots about your mother and her youth, quite a bit about your father and lots and lots and lots about USA history, but not really very much about yourself." Anni had wondered about this before, as Brian's 1949 comments show: "You say, when is the 'Job-in-hand' coming down to you and me? It has, my darling, in my letters to you. If I die too soon, regard them as part of it." Brian was confident that the letters were good. "Some day, when we are dead, someone will find our letters and read them and think, they're rather wonderful and make a book of most of what's in them," he said in 1946. And yet, after his death, Anni felt unsure and confused.

She even made an attempt to write about the women in Brian's life – his "harem", as she put it, but felt unable to complete Brian's project. "You, my darling, had such a wonderful photographic memory and mine has never been good. I've always been superficial, so is also my memory." She was also able to explain away Brian's string of lovers. "You were so good, essentially good and so steadfast – no matter that you had mistress after mistress – it was your Olympian background – your belief in Greek gods and ancient Greek ways. But you were true to your principles and did whatever the cost, what you thought right. I'm very proud of course that once we became lovers you never had another mistress – I was the only one for over 30 years."

So how did these two people, the domineering Brian and submissive Anni, come to be attracted to each other in the first place, let alone fall in love and live happily ever after? They seem so different, and yet Brian exerted his influence even from the grave: Anni declared a need to read Caesar's *The Gallic Wars* and Xenophon's *The Persian Expedition* that she had not had time for in Brian's lifetime. In years gone by, Brian had been gratified whenever Anni read the books he had recommended. "I'm more than pleased, I'm really happy that you love *The Odyssey* – it's so big a part of my mental, emotional, moral and spiritual background, and Lawrence's translation is as perfect as translation can be. Next time, instead of reading you W.W. Jacobs, Ansty, Stevenson, Weyman, Lock I will – if it suits you, read you one of Shakespeare's plays, and then the New Testament. You will come to love them too, but both should be read to you. Shakespeare, because he is hard to grasp unaided – with hardly a line of stage-directions it is most difficult to visualise the whole thing. And I would love to read you the New Testament because I know and love it so. I refer to the four Gospels."

Brian was so pleased that Anni couldn't put down *The Odyssey* that he returned to the subject. "It is a deep personal happiness to me, for I was brought up on Homer and Hellenism – *The Odyssey* is part of the woof and pattern of my background, and it is to me as if, in a great place of my own I had a special and dearest little garden, and you had – at last – come into it and just adored it."

The couple had their quarrels. Anni had a fiery temper and this at times caused problems; some of the quarrels were about Brian's first wife Claire. Theirs was a *ménage à trois* of a curious kind because it included Claire, also known as Bee. The inclusion was sexless, more to do with belonging, and yet it disturbed Anni. "I know you said you never told me a lie," Anni told her diary/Brian in 1968, after Brian's death; "you did not need to tell me a lie, very likely you thought you loved me more than anyone else, but to the end you worried about your having failed Bee and asked for her forgiveness, even ten years after her death." (Claire died in 1957.)

When in 1954 Anni went to Sweden to visit her mother and sisters, Brian stayed with Claire for a couple of weeks and afterwards thanked her by letter. "Anni and I are terribly grateful to you. Anni feels that nowhere could I relax as perfectly as with you – rest, fresh air and going at it slowly – first – exercise, and get really fit. It'll be lovely giving you all our news and hearing yours. I could not afford to go anywhere else and we both dreaded the idea of my spending my leave at home."

In 1945 Claire was the one to admonish Brian to take proper care of Anni: "She is devoted to you, and lives only for you," Claire said. "Three women before her have loved you with a love as deep, but you were not able to appreciate them. The first you lost – the other two you made very unhappy. Guard this great happiness well that God has once more given you!" Meanwhile Brian told Anni that he couldn't exist without her, "for I am so entirely yours that I have no longer a separate existence. And that is why I always pray and still hope that you may come to feel full understanding, much sympathy and a certain tolerant affection for her [Claire]. If you cannot, I shall indeed be sad."

When in summer of 1946 Brian had only two weeks of leave, he wanted to spend a day with Claire. "Would you be so generous and give most of one day of our leave to Claire?" he asked Anni, making her part of the plan. "Preferably by asking her up to London." Anni decided to buy a set of records of a piano concerto by Tchaikovsky for Claire as a birthday present and Brian praised her for it, saying it "was one of the loveliest things even you have ever done. You are indeed a woman of magnificent gestures... My goodness, I am proud of you!" His habit of buying cases of wine for Claire continued for years (in addition to paying her a monthly allowance ever since their divorce).

As if the idea of a threesome wasn't bad enough, Brian wanted some kindness spared for Nadja, his former mistress, and in 1946 urged Anni to invite her to town. "She is desperately lonely, really homesick and often very unhappy," he said. "And you, if she can feel that you are her real friend, can be a tower of strength and comfort to her." Once the two women had met, Brian told Anni how pleased he was: "Never has anyone I know well made a more magnificent showing, or done more to give happiness or, as far as I can judge, succeed."

50. Anni Giffey.

Most of Brian's surviving letters were love letters. He was enthusiastic and fervent, as he was about most things in life. "My dear, you are not only beautiful – you are exquisite," he told Anni. "I have gained the love, the passionate love even, and married a nymph of Ancient Hellas...I will learn to draw and paint as I never have before, if only to do justice to your beauty, your entire loveliness, and to our passionate love." He declared: "Love of you has changed me – it seems impossible that it's almost eleven years since you became the only woman that really mattered to me."

Brian's letters were to support Anni from afar and keep their relationship alive. "I expect most couples, in the first flush of happy and reciprocated love, in that sweet exaltation of perfect sentimental, physical and – in the best – spiritual harmony that is young love – if it be their first great love – imagine that they love as few, if any, have ever loved before. But we, my Heart, – at 59 and 34 – after more than eleven years of perfect love and passion, perfect friendship and comradeship, adventure and romance can say indeed that there have been few loves as ours. We had our supreme periods, in one aspect or another, but none seem to me to have been as perfect and exquisite, as truly lovely or to have filled our lives with music as our last leave and the present spring. Even our present pain of separation and our longing seem to me exquisitely sweet pain, with more than a promise of solace and fulfilment and of ideal comradeship to come."

After twelve days of London leave Brian wrote from Berlin: "You know I don't agree with you, Lovely, that the happiest times pass quickly, as a dream, and seem short, and even unreal, in retrospect. On the contrary, when a time was full of beauty and gladness, so many hours, so many beautiful moments, are so deeply impressed on my mind and ever before me that the time seems longer than it really was. Laden with happiness it feels as if it had been three weeks rather than twelve days. I am still deeply under its influence and devotedly grateful to the Gods and you, my Beautiful, for so much beauty, so much joy, and so much tender happiness. Much though I long for you I am still happy in retrospect, and the memory of that wonderful time, and the extra day, one of the days of purest unspoilt gold." On another occasion he said: "I think that people who see us together will always think we're on our honeymoon."

It would be only fair to include at least one poem he composed for Anni (as he had done previously for Claire and others). The one below was written for Valentine's Day in 1948; it looked back on the happiness they had known in Tallinn:

"The winter's sun tried hard to shine
On that cold day, Sweetheart mine
Thirteen years ago –
On the brink of loving still
We walked on Tallinn's Castle Hill
Amid ice and snow.
Daintily you tripped ahead
With light and certain fairy tread
Down to the frozen moat,
And with fresh and tinkling laugh
Watched me tobogganing down the path
Sitting on my coat.
Close we later sat
Talking of this and that
Spoke soft and low,
Thrilling us through and through
As with roseate glow
Love within us grew,
Wrapping us closely furled
In a sweet magic world
World of our own
Yours and mine alone
Then began, Sweetheart mine
Our first, lovely Valentine."[2]

"The world is ours in partnership," Brian told Anni. "For we work together, play together, run, sail, row, swim, play games together and adore travel and adventure, trees, mountains and the sea, fresh air and exercise. Both we love our friends and are interested in everybody, love meeting foreign people and learning languages. You've taught me to love flowers, I taught you to love ships. I design your clothes, and you love to have them, and even wear them, and you choose my ties and shirts and socks, and make and mend them. I think your cookery is divine, and you my painting wonderful. We both love fun and laughter, but thrill to the same enthusiasms, to all things beautiful, and most of all perhaps to pity, and we both love to help all whom we can. We draw together and love books, love music, films and plays, are mad on dancing and delight in naked love and shameless passion. Indeed we're marvellously alike."[3]

Even their differences might be an advantage, Brian told Anni: "It is good that I should be an enthusiast, venturesome and always ready to take chances, and that you should be cautious, diffident, point out the possible disadvantages and dangers even for risking this and that, and of proposals which I might lightheartedly accept." Anni delighted in the fact that Brian was a born gentleman who had "kindness and gentleness and your old-world courtesy and dignity."

"What a good companion Brian is," she wrote. "He is so good in himself – so lovable. Everyone likes him and I love him more than I can say. I do wish I could make him really happy always – I succeed sometimes, as now – we are so happy. There is nothing like the thrill to hear and see him entering the room – our room – he belongs to me – I belong to him – his happy smile, his caressing arms, his fond kisses – and the peace to be with him anywhere – always – he's so full of life and schemes and dreams – he's so clever. How is it that he of all people loves me, chose me to be his companion and mistress and wife – poor, small, nothing to look at and so terribly shy. He could have picked or chosen any other girl – and I can't even give him a child what is his real desire – a child, a boy – and I'm barren," Anni lamented.[4]

In many ways Anni and Brian were well matched. She delighted in him being "always so absolutely superior to me" while he was often patronising. He always knew what she should do, she mostly accepted his judgement and was pleased to receive praise for her actions afterwards. There was something Pygmalion-like in Brian's designs. She was young and Brian took an interest in her development. In 1946 he predicted that she might one day become "a very great writer, or even an artist, or God knows what." He told her: "You had infinite possibilities and though you rate yourself too low (a good thing perhaps!) and me much too high (and not a bad thing either!!) I do agree with you so far that I was the best man for you, and perhaps the most suited to assist your development." Six years later Brian told a friend: "Anni has turned into a remarkably fine housewife, you know, and into a really magnificent cook – the slang word 'wizzard' just fairly describes what she can produce with the simplest means." This lowering of expectation makes one wince.

Anni's job was to look after Brian and their home, which she happily accepted. Apart from a couple of months in Tallinn and Helsinki in 1939-40 and a period of eleven months in wartime London, Anni never had a full-time job. It's amusing, and sad, how often she told her diary of the number of Brian's socks that needed darning.

But when in 1949 Anni wanted to attend a course at the Royal School of Needlework the couple had a major disagreement.

She had always been clever with the needle, but Brian got cold feet. He reminded her of 1941-42 when she worked for C (Brian called him Bill elsewhere) in SOE: "We'll have to discuss the School at length. I've been used to long regular hours and discipline all my life, you have not. And 11 months under C, who was an irritating boss, but an easy one, was too much for you. Typing and shorthand ditto.You'd be tired out, often short-tempered, and we'd be unhappy again. Who'd do the housework (which the char can't do), meals, washing up, all the little bits of this and that, shopping? I think we'll have to stick to it that I work and paint and do the big business, and you do the housekeeping and shopping."

51. Anni taught embroidery class two evenings a week in 1956.

Brian had more to add: "The more I think of the school, the less do I like it. It would strain your eyes and temper, give you headaches and make us miserable. I'm so happy to see you fitter now than you've ever been and it'd worry me to a frazzle to see you tired out. Don't risk your health and our happiness.

How can we both work all day and have a home worth the name? You make and keep us a happy home and appetising meals and do all the shopping that belongs to it while I work."

Anni must have finally persuaded him because he had a change of heart. Two years later when she completed the course and obtained a diploma, Brian was very proud of her. "I hope she hasn't been too modest to give you an idea how splendidly she has done at the RSN," he told a friend. Her studies took her away from home two full days a week and she also taught two evening classes in term time.[5] "And with it all she is perfectly happy, serene and contented, happier even I think than when we were so well off in Tallinn and later in the Police," Brian noted.[6] He knew that the RSN was also satisfied. "They particularly like her neat embroidery, but most of all her design, colour sense and rhythm in her drawing and painting." His conclusion was that "Anni's joining the RSN has been the most important thing in her life, and I'm terribly happy about it."[7]

She was one of the number of (unidentified) women to work on the Queen's coronation robes and in 1953, as a sign of recognition, she was invited to a garden party at Buckingham Palace. Brian was not invited but had comments to make. He wished that the Queen would keep her girlishness. As to her consort, he made extravagant comparisons: "The Duke, Philip, competes in my mind with Xenophon for first place. He completely fills the eye and satisfies the heart."

Brian habitually made unexpected references to the United States, a country he probably never visited. Travelling on a paddle steamer near Basra in Mesopotamia in 1917, he noticed the steamy heat: "The whole atmosphere [is] reminiscent of cotton and rice fields, plantations and negroes, of ilex and acacia, the broad Mississipi and the voyage from St Louis to New Orleans." Impressed with the swashbuckling hero Alan

Breck Stewart of Robert Louis Stevenson's *Kidnapped*, Brian sometimes called himself Alan Brec Gordon. And Anni by extension referred to herself as Mrs Alan Gordon.

Brian was a man of surprise. He drew a whole book of semi-pornographic sketches, loved wearing shorts and enjoyed naked sunbathing, but he also joined the Royal Rose Lodge in London. He hated being ill because this never happened to Homeric heroes. Among other things he told his diary: "Though I shouldn't tell everybody by a long chalk, I firmly believe in reincarnation, and fancy that I remember some things of what I believe was my last, as an officer of the CSA [Confederate States Army] from Alabama, in greater detail and with tenderer force than some matters in my present life. And this cannot be explained by heredity or outside influence, as my Cavalier propensities and general impressions of the period of Kings Charles I and II could. An awfully fascinating subject, the whole thing."[8]

He liked righteous declarations. "Moral independence is the greatest possession on earth. That torch of essential individual Liberty that was first lit in Hellas. Of which the American Constitution sings. How deep the love of it is planted in the Briton, and in the Estonian heart." When Anni was about to join him in Berlin in 1947, he told her: "We shall be privileged to make and share in making history of the most vital importance to the future of the world, privileged to have the most wonderful experience, privileged to help and serve: to serve and help our country, and poor humanity, beyond the power most people obtain, and opportunity most people ever get, if we observe the rules and make ourselves pleasant to all we shall have a wonderful time, and we shall be together, Lovely, at last."

And yet I feel that he never quite fitted in: he tried, but didn't quite make it. He told Anni in 1946 "that the odds have always been, slightly at most times and sometimes heavily, against me. That I've been a bit of an outsider most of my life everywhere where I felt that I belonged and, in the main, wanted most of all but to serve, that I've been in many a tight corner, often afraid, and sometimes utterly disheartened. You see, Lovely, to you I seemed rather a splendid figure and frightfully strong. True, I'm a pretty good fighter when I fight for others, and in latter years I have – touching wood – been luckier. I'm not so good when fighting for my own hand. My greatest strength is still my enthusiasms, and that's quite all right. But, having known me 12 years only you wouldn't know how I've had to fight, and how hard to work, for every step I've gained." Anni, too, saw him as an outsider. He may have even wanted to be one.

Brian was very proud of his military career (and membership of the Naval and Military Club) but there, too, things didn't always go smoothly, supporting the argument that he perhaps wanted to be an outsider. When he arrived on a training course in 1924 with a very poor confidental report, Maj-Gen C. Fielding was immediately wary, but later wondered how the report had come about, since he had nothing but praise for Brian. And what is one to make of a fellow officer's comment that Brian was "not a typical soldier in looks or outlook"? Much as Brian wanted to be English, his first 19 years in Germany must have left a mark on his habits and manner.

Having been made redundant at the age of 62, Brian was bitter to be "too old". He craved recognition, but it often eluded him. "I never reached the rank of full Colonel. I hold no decoration," he said sadly. "But I bear honourable wounds of war, I was given accelerated promotion, I am liked and respected, I think, by all I know... I am content," said the optimist in him. Ambitious yet somehow deficient, Brian wrote: "One of the proudest moments of my life was when I was 59 and C's friend, after some hours of travelling in company, assumed as a matter of course that I was commanding Our Battalion in Germany."

52. Anni and Brian celebrate with a cake in the 1960s.

Never careful with money, finances were very much on Brian's mind as he was getting older. "And I shall live and die a poor man and probably a very poor man," he said at one point.[9] He told Anni: "Having seen me and shared my life, as a sort of diplomat and as a soldier... and been so happy in the wide sweep and the big glamorous and engrossing business of all that life, it may hurt you to see me disregarded, patronised, ordered about and pushed about by the stupid and the vulgar. I also am a little sad. What glamour, interest, romance, splendour, even adventure – not to speak of ease, elegance and comfort, comparative wealth even and, certainly, position was I not able to give you in the past. And now – in 18 months, or less, we shall have to start counting every penny. And we shall have no position whatever." This almost maudlin view overlooked the fact that in Iraq, for example, they didn't exactly have ease, elegance and comfort.

In 1952, when Brian was working for the Ukrainians in a poorly-paid job, he won £62.12.6 in a club sweep. He was delighted that "that grand horse Tulyar" had done them proud at Doncaster. "Our money worries until Christmas (incl.) are over," he told Anni in September. "This will provide for the Insurance of our gear in November, clear my overdraft, pay my 1st October subscription, we can both have our shoes repaired, and you shall have a new pair of stockings and the material you wanted. Thank God. Amen."[10] Is it really possible that without this windfall the Giffeys would have had no decent shoes? This might be yet another exaggeration; in actual fact Brian gave Anni a cheque for £4 to buy a brand new pair.

Anni too worried about money. When offered to teach embroidery in evening class she rejoiced: "And now I'm going to earn a very little each week. That too is a help and we do not need to worry, worry, worry about money."[11] Brian the provider worried even at the age of 71, in 1958, in connection with Anni's teaching. "I wish I could earn or win enough to save you having to go to work at all," he said wistfully.

Few people have described Brian. MI6 files have him as "an eccentric individual who flies off at a tangent and is difficult to pin down." One of his colleagues, David Mure, remarked that Brian was hardly a reliable source.[12] On the other hand, Brian's boss (whom Brian called "Big Brother") was satisfied with him in 1941-42 when he was section chief in charge of gathering information on the Soviets: Brian had a thorough approach and thought things through, he said. His methods were not the quickest, but they produced results.[13]

Brian was undoubtedly a marvellous storyteller, but in his writing he was often wordy, long-winded and undisciplined. I have mourned the loss of his diaries while wondering whether I'd be able to read thousands of pages of his prose. The one surviving diary runs to 400 pages but covers only two months of his life. He wrote "a south sea romance" called *Alota* and it may well be a blessing that no trace of it has been found. Apart from a letter to *The Times* published in 1919 and two Taras Shevchenko poems translated from the Ukrainian in the 1950s no other publication has come to light.[14] He certainly was a capable man, as shown by his painstaking work in post-war Berlin to hammer out the denazification directive and other quadripartite documents – undoubtedly his biggest known achievement – but at times his enthusiasm ran away with him.

Brian lived to the ripe old age of 80. Anni was only 55 when he died. Taking sleeping pills and "nerve pills", she briefly contemplated moving to Stockholm to join her sister, but then decided in favour of independence and continued to live at 78 Southwold Mansions. Not even having a television, she gradually became a recluse, as Brian had predicted in 1945: "That, my Sweet, is your danger in life, retirement within yourself, your own thoughts and interests. You would belong to nothing and serve no one, no cause, and that would be a pity, for service is what makes life worth having lived."

Brian certainly gave good service. He was gregarious and his ideas of other people were often daft, as his obituary in the regimental newspaper *Firm* demostrates. I think he might chuckle in his present reincarnation if he knew that he has been remembered as follows: "Never a great athlete, he nevertheless gave every encouragement to his soldiers at games, and anyone who served in his Company will remember the occasion when on a Company cross-country run in Rhine Army he set off walking with a 15-minute start, and promised his men 5 Marks each if they passed him. Needless to say the soldiers took every possible short cut and cost him a fortune! It is also recorded that he once turned out for cricket and achieved the unique distinction, as reported in the 'Cologne Post' at the time, of being 'caught off the tail of his shirt'."[15]

What might have been Brian's own final words? A man of contradictions, noble ideals, determination and appreciation of the arts, he may have chosen the sentences he once wrote to Anni: "One must never, never lose control. Power. Power to do good. Power to create what is beautiful and fine, and in the end, to give much happiness, is good. And thus will I try to grow powerful. First in myself. That has been the message "Caesar and Cleopatra" [by Bernard Shaw] has given me."

Or his final words may have been about Kim Philby. However, there is no quote, not a scrap of evidence to present. Philby is not mentioned in any of Brian's surviving papers; there is not even a newspaper cutting among his papers from 1963 when the notorious spy fled to Moscow. This is odd, in the light of the old Baghdad receipts, water bills and Cairo hotel bills that have travelled, yet survived. To me Brian seems to have been a hoarder. He kept the rules for Alwiyah Club in Baghdad, left comments on Stewart Perowne's communist views, and yet among his papers there are hardly any letters from his friends. Did they not discuss the flight of Burgess and Maclean in 1951? Did they not refer to Philby after 1963?

Brian was by then just a pensioner, but Philby's treachery must have affected him deeply. Or was he still worried about money, concerned that Anni might face hardship in widowhood? That anything referring to his work might be making life harder for her when he was gone? That she might be deprived of a pension? He died without making a will, but Anni had savings of £1,000 plus an army pension of £9 a week. Her rent and bills came to £6 a week, but in 1971 there was a sharp rent increase and she contemplated moving into the countryside, and yet she died in 2000 in the same old London flat.

Is it likely that Anni who was utterly devoted to Brian would have decided to destroy his papers? She even asked her sister Totti in Sweden to burn the letters they had sent to her. "I do think when I've cleaned the flat and got everything in order, then my task is done," she wrote in 1968. And yet an odd assortment of papers did survive. One possible explanation may have something to do with her will in which she mysteriously left £25,000. Could she have been paid to destroy the papers? If you, dear reader, have something to add to this mystery, or to Brian's life story, please email: tinatamman@yahoo.co.uk

Brian died a long time ago but the countries he knew well – Russia and Iraq – are still in the news. Estonia, another country he knew, is fearful about its future after Russia's recent annexation of Crimea; the events of 1940 are well remembered there. Today's Russia is different from the Soviet Union, but the country wants to be a big player and has the capacity to confuse the West. Meanwhile MI6 archives remain closed and new espionage books focus on the persons and incidents already in the public domain. History, however, is all about human beings.

Notes

Introduction

1   Jeffery, 2010, p. viii.
2   Ibid., p. 191.
3   West, 1987, p. 322; see also West and Tsarev, 2009, p. 352 for Frank Giffey.
4   Tomaselli, 2009, pp. 113, 178.
5   Compare Philby, 1968, p. 38 and *My Silent*, 1968, p. 21.
6   *My Silent*, 1968, p. 14.
7   Jeffrey, 2010, p. x.
8   Wark, 1996, p. 642; Nicholson's memoirs were published under the pseudonym of John Whitwell in 1966.
9   Peter Hennessy, "Disclosure of British war secrets allowed", *The Times*, 10.5.1977.
10 Letters to the editor, *The Times*, 24.5.1977.
11 Peter Hennessy, "Disclosures 'would have horrified MI6 chief'", *The Times*, 1.6.1977.
12 Richard Clogg, "Nigel Clive, intelligence officer whose memoirs preceded Spycatcher", *The Guardian*, 18.5.2001. The autobiographies in question are: John Whitwell, *British Agent*; Kim Philby, *My Silent War*; Peggie Benton, *Baltic Countdown*; David Mure, *Practise to Deceive* and Nigel Clive, *A Greek Experience 1943-1948*.
13 Jeffery, 2010, p. x.
14 Creedy of War Office to FO 6.10.1939, Cadogan to Creedy 15.10.1939 TNA FO 371/24049 W14500/13457/50.
15 British embassy in Baghdad to William Hayter 4.12.1947 TNA FO 1093/368.
16 Ibid.

17 CHMW memo 23.6.1942 TNA CAB 301/97.

18 Government Communications Bureau to Brian 14.12.1967
    Stockholm Colection. For the non-existence of the bureau see
    Martin Bright and Tim Kalvis, "Charity HQ blocked by spy
    bureau", *The Observer*, 8.9.2002 and Jason Lewis, "Secret fund
    for retired spy care homes is hit by credit crunch", *Mail on
    Sunday*, 2.8.2008.

19 F.J. Waters of FO to Brian 24.1.1949 Stockholm Collection.

20 Paas, 1974, pp. 42, 95.

Chapter 1 Beginnings

1 Blunck, 1953, p. 83.

2 Ibid., p. 94.

3 Ibid.

4 Ibid., p. 85.

5 Ibid., pp. 85-86.

6 Ibid., p. 84.

7 See Chester Gorton's naturalisation papers March 1868 TNA
   HO 1/147/5733.

8 "Orders made on applications for discharge",
   The London Gazette, 26.1.1892.

9 Gregory, 1929, p. 5.

10 Oxford University records UR 1/2/62; *The Times*, 1.12.1911.

Chapter 2 Wounded in Flanders

1 Stacke, 2002, p. xxvii.

2 Ibid., p. 52.

3 Barton, 1976, p. 92.

4 Ibid., pp. 89-91.

5 Blunck, 1953, p. 97.

6 See Stacke, 2002, p. 125 for a description of the day.

Chapter 3 Heat and dust of Mesopotamia

1 See description of the battle at Kut in Stacke, 2002, p. 220.

Chapter 4   Travel and training years

1   Lauri Kopisto, "The British Intervention in South Russia 1918-1920", unpublished dissertation 2011, https://helda.helsinki.fi/bitstream/handle/10138/26041/thebriti.pdf?, p. 73.
2   "Denikin as a leader. A man of the people. Three weeks' conquests." *The Times*, 21.6.1919.
3   "Freed from the Red terror. A tour in liberated Russia. Value of British aid." *The Times*, 23.8.1919.
4   TNA WO 95/4959 and Brian Giffey's service form B199A from APC.
5   Maj-Gen Holman's report Oct 1918-March 1920 TNA WO 33/971.
6   Birdwood, 1953, p. 103.
7   Barton, 1976, p. 94.

Chapter 5   Secret agent in Tallinn

1   Lloyds Bank to Brian 20.9.1928 Stockholm Collection.
2   Whitwell, 1966, pp. 19-20.
3   Director of Passport Control in London to Giffey 18.12.1928 Stockholm Collection.
4   Andrew, 1992, pp. 347-50, 408.
5   Jeffery, 2010, p. 184.
6   Tolley, 1983, p. 35.
7   Greene, 2008, p. 62.
8   Mockler, 1994, p. 94.
9   Walter, 1999, pp. 133-34.
10   Laaman's diary 2.2.1926 ERA 827/1/6b.
11   "Estonia and the Soviets. A renegade minister", *The Times*, 16.7.1926.
12   Laaman's diary 2.2.1926 ERA 827/1/6b; "Soviet espionage trial", *Evening Standard*, 20.2.1926.
13   I. Kondurushkin, "Vyvody iz protsessa 48 shpionov" (Conclusions of the 48 spies' trial), *Leningradskaya Pravda*, 20.2.1926.
14   Niidassoo and Ohmann, 2000, p. 69.
15   Estonian political police report 11.12.1935 ERA 957/14/161.

16 Undated KGB report, probably 1934 ERAF 138SM/1/42.

17 Whitwell, 1966, p. 59-60.

18 Salza's interrogation notes 9.2.1932 ERA 927/1/710.

19 Leading personalities in Estonia 15.1.1932 TNA FO 371/16263 N545/5/59.

20 Haritonov's interrogation notes 9.2.1932 ERA 927/1/710.

21 Jeffery, 2010, pp. 188-91.

22 Haritonov's KGB file 1940-41 ERAF 129SM/1/26736.

23 Rudolf Stilling's files ERA 927/1/696, 927/1/697, 852/1/377 and 1356/4/211.

24 Jeffery, 2010, p. 604; *Aruanne*, 1997, p. 17.

25 Estonian KGB 1946 report ERAF 131SM/1/39; West and Tsarev, 2009, p. 330. The numbers went with the post and therefore 43317 denoted also Eduard-Johannes Aavik, head of the shipping directorate – see *Aruanne*, 1997, p. 32. Similarly, 43281 belonged also to Ferdinand Schmiedehelm – see p. 33.

26 Reports dated January 1933 and 21.2.1933 ERAF 138SM/1/53.

27 For more information on Reilly's entrapment see Lucas, 2012, pp. 209-11.

28 Internal KGB letters 7.6.1935, 13.6.1935, 8.8.1935; agent reports 17.8.1936 and 18.8.-1.9.1936 ERAF SM/1/53.

29 For more detail on Roman Birk see Tamman, 2011, p. 45.

30 Report dated 30.11.1932 ERAF 138SM/1/53.

31 Report on British intelligence in Estonia 5.9.1933 ERAF 138SM/1/53.

32 Shipp's report 27.1.1933 NARA RG165 Military Intelligence Division 9944-DD-2/2.

33 Shipp's report 12.10.1932 NARA RG165 Military Intelligence Division 9944-DD-2/1.

34 Ibid.

35 Shipp's report 27.1.1933 NARA RG165 Military Intelligence Division 9944-DD-2/2 and 12. 10.1932 NARA RG165 Military Intelligence Division 9944-DD-2/1.

36 Report on British intelligence in Estonia 5.9.1933 ERAF 138SM/1/53.

37 Undated FO memo TNA KV 2/2404.

38 FO memo 29.10.1934 TNA KV 2/2404.

39 Jeffery, 2010, p. 554; Maasing's file ERAF 138SM/1/8.

40   West and Tsarev, 1999, p. 303; West and Tsarev, 2009, pp. 329-30.

41   Estonian KGB 1946 report ERAF 131SM/1/39; Richard Maasing's file ERAF 138SM/1/8.

42   *Aruanne*, 1997, p. 32.

43   Stirling, 2005, pp. 182, 551. The KGB knew that 98 Polish agents were operating in Estonia up until 1940 – see *Aruanne*, 1997, p. 19.

44   Note June 1940 ERAF 138SM/1/42.

45   Estonian KGB report to Moscow 13.1.1947 ERAF 131SM/1/39; West and Tsarev, 2009, p. 330.

46   Benton, 1984, p. 102.

47   Whitwell, 1966, pp. 74, 69.

48   Edgar Pillov's charge sheet 8.6.1945 and interrogation records 27.2.1946 ERAF 129SM/1/16011.

49   J.E.S. Cooper's reminiscences TNA HW 3/83; files HW 61/46 and 61/49 on Estonian liaison and Craig Graham McKay, "British SIGINT and the Bear, 1919-1941. Some discoveries in the GC&CS archive", www.kkrva.se/Artiklar/972/british_sigint.html

50   *Aruanne*, 1997, pp. 53-54.

51   West and Tsarev, 2009, p. 330. The report is dated April 1943 but is retrospective.

52   Sooman's interrogation records 24.3.41 ERAF 138SM/1/8.

53   Anni to Ants 7.8.1943 and 23.5.1945 EKN EKLA 237/M53:3; West and Tsarev, 2009, p. 239; *Aruanne*, 1997, p. 60.

54   List on potential Soviet recruits in Estonia 4.9.1935 ERAF 138SM/1/42.

55   Ilmjärv, 1999, p. 122.

56   Jeffery, 2010, p. 604.

57   *The Times*, 23.12.1931; *Firm*, Jan 1932, p. 356.

Chapter 6   Love is in the air

1   Roolaht, 1990, p. 268.

2   Stacke, 2002, p. 503.

3   Claire Marie Therese Giffey vs Chester Kenneth Otho Brian Giffey 1936-37 TNA J 77/3696/9755.

4   Seljamaa to missions 3.8.1934 ERA 957/13/764.

5   Parliamentary foreign affairs committee minutes 24.1.1939 ERA 957/18/34; Eduard Laaman's diary 26.8.1939 ERA 827/1/6b.

6   Laaman's diary 14.9.1939 ERA 827/1/6b.

7   Pullat, 2001, pp. 160-163; www.orzel.one.pl/viewpage. php?page_id=25; Roolaht, 1990, pp. 316-17; Luts, 2004, pp. 74-75; Stirling, 2005, p. 177.

8   Gallienne to London 17.11.1939 TNA FO 371/23610 N6993/4898/59.

9   Benton, 1984, p. 73.

10 Gallienne to London 23.9.1939 TNA FO 371/23610 N4898/4898/59.

11 Gallienne to London 13.11.1939 TNA FO 371/23610 N6561/5099/59.

12 Ibid.

13 Gallienne to London 15.2.1940 TNA FO 371/24765 N2484/2484/59.

14 Orde to London 5.12.1939 TNA FO 371/23610.

15 "Resident British minister appointed to Tallinn", *The Baltic Times*, Tallinn, 26.4.1940.

16 FO minute 26.3.1940 TNA FO 371/24765 N3628/3628/59.

17 Gallienne to London 24.7.1940 TNA FO 371/24761 N6045/1224/59.

18 Ibid.

Chapter 7   Flight from Tallinn

1   Gallienne to London 23.9.1939 TNA FO 371/23610 N4898/4898/59.

2   *Aruanne*, 1998, p. 57.

3   West and Tsarev, 2009, p. 330.

4   Brian to Ants 13.6.1943 EKM EKLA 237/M53:3.

5   Reference from "Söhnchen" in London 20.3.1942 ERAF 138SM/1/8.

6   Tarvel, 1999, pp. 6-7.

7   Typing errors were common, so the figure may have been 65 for Estonia. See West and Tsarev, 2009, p. 329.

8   Estonian KGB report to Moscow 13.1.1948 ERAF 131SM/1/120.

9   Jürjo, 1996, pp. 66-67.

10   Estonian consul-general in Leningrad to Estonian Foreign
      Ministry 28.7.1933 ERA 957/13/755.
11   Estonian KGB annual report to Moscow 14.1.1956 ERAF
      131SM/1/318 and 12.1.1957 ERAF 131SM/1/358.
12   Estonian KGB annual report to Moscow 31.3.1955 ERAF
      131SM/1/319.
13   Estonian KGB annual report to Moscow 12.1.1957 ERAF
      131SM/1/358.
14   KGB notes Oct 1946, 20.4.1948, 18.10.1949 ERAF 138SM/1/8;
      Jürjo, 1996, p. 70.
15   Estonian KGB reports to Moscow office 18.4.1950 and 2.10.1950
      ERAF 138SM/1/8.
16   Wolff and Moullec, 2005, p. 92.
17   Andrew and Gordievsky, 1991, pp. 389-90; Philby, 1968, p. 199.
18   Estonian KGB annual report to Moscow 31.3.1955 ERAF
      131SM/1/319.
19   *Aruanne*, 1997, p. 55.
20   Mothander, 1998, p. 225.

Chapter 8   Destination Baghdad

1   Gallienne to Brian 23.5.1942 Stockholm Collection.
2   West and Tsarev, 1999, pp. 302, 305.
3   KGB note 17.3.1945 ERAF 138SM/1/8; Jeffery, 2010, p. 554.
4   Stirling, 2005, p. 287.
5   Jeffery, 2010, p. 562; West and Tsarev, 1999, p. 305; Mockler,
      1994, p. 195.
6   Smith, 1999, p. 235.
7   Macintyre, 2014, pp. 1, 29.
8   Greene, 2008, p. 412; Greene, 1999, p. 299; Mockler, 1994, p. 196.
9   Tamman, 2011, pp. 173-74.
10   The uncatalogued papers were mentioned in Dovey, 1993, p. 60.
11   Pownall's report 12.10.1943 TNA FO 371/39979 E122/12/65.
12   Propaganda plan for Iraq 24.2.1943 TNA FO 371/35014
      E1119/914/93.
13   Anni to Ants and Liivi 8.11.1943 EKM EKLA 237/M53:3.
14   Anni to Ants and Liivi 16.9.1943 EKM EKLA 237/M53:3.
15   CICI to embassy in Baghdad 1.2.1943 TNA FO 624/32, Swiss
      file.

16 British embassy in Cairo to embassy in Baghdad 4.2.1943 TNA
    FO 624/32/279.
17 File on Gyula Kovacs TNA KV 2/2849.
18 Original letter in Arabic 28.1.1943 circulated in English
    translation 16.2.1943 TNA FO 624/31.
19 Knatchbull-Hugessen in Ankara to Cornwallis in Baghdad
    24.2.1943 TNA FO 624/31.
20 Censor's special summary 13.2.1943 and GHQ Middle East
    Forces to embassy in Baghdad 10.3.1943 TNA FO 624/32/279,
    Egypt file.
21 Stirling, 2005, pp. 372-73, 378; Pullat, 2001, p. 266.
22 Stirling, 2005, p. 373.
23 West and Tsarev, 2009, pp. 150-51.
24 Andrew and Mitrokhin, 2005, p. 169.
25 West and Tsarev, 2009, p. 318.
26 Cornwallis to Eden 22.1.1943 TNA FO 371/35010 E946/489/93.
27 See chapter on Fahd in Batatu, 1978, pp. 485-492.
28 Anni to Ants and Liivi 8.11.1943 EKM EKLA 237/M53:3.
29 Anni to Ants and Liivi 16.9.1943 EKM EKLA 237/M53:3.
30 PICME report 28.7.1943 TNA FO 624/34.
31 Thompson of British embassy in Baghdad to Hamilton of
    the Office of the Minister of State in Cairo 25.7.1943 TNA FO
    624/34.
32 Clive, 1985, pp. 20-21.
33 Ibid., pp. 18-21; West, 2009, p. 99.
34 Jeffery, 2010, pp. 421, 503; Clive, 1985, p. 19; British embassy to
    William Hayter of FO 4.12.1947 TNA FO 1093/368.
35 West and Tsarev, 2009, pp. 150-52.
36 British embassy in Baghdad to William Hayter in FO 4.12.1947
    TNA FO 1093/368.
37 West and Tsarev, 2009, pp. 151-52.
38 Anni to Ants and Liivi 7.8.1943 EKN EKLA 237/M53:3.
39 Anni to Ants and Liivi 16.9.-4.10.1943 EKM EKLA 237/M53:3.
40 For an excellent analysis of the Kurdish problem see Wichhart,
    2011, pp. 815-31.
41 Cornwallis to Eden 12.11.1943 TNA FO 371/35013
    E7407/489/93; Thompson to London 11.12.1943 TNA FO
    371/35013.

42 Cornwallis to London 25.4.43 TNA FO 371/35020; 13.12.1943
    TNA FO 371/35013 E7823/489/93; 9.1.45 TNA FO 371/45302
    E608/195/93.
43 FO to Baghdad 24.12.1943 TNA FO 371/35013 E8045/489/93.
44 *Stepan*, 1999, pp. 109-10.
45 Pownall to War Office 12.10.1943 TNA FO 371/39979
    E122/12/65.

Chapter 9   Dismissed from intelligence service

1   Anni's diary 9.2.1944 Stockholm Collection.
2   Anni's diary 26.2.1944 Stockholm Collection.
3   Wharry to Brian 18.3.1944 Stockholm Collection.
4   Brig Allen's minute 23.5.1944 and Brig Maunsell to Brig Petrie
    7.6.1944 TNA KV 4/223.
5   Brian to Ants Oras 1.9.1944 EKN EKLA 237/M53:3.
6   Jeffery, 2010, p. 261; Philby, 1968, p. 128.
7   Mockler, 1994, pp. 192-93.
8   Obituary of Sir Dick White 23.2.1993, *Washington Post*, provides
    an example of the manner in which the word "dismissal" was
    avoided.
9   Undated history TNA KV 4/223; London to Baghdad 15.7.1941
    CAB 301/97.
10 Loxley of FO to Brittain of Treasury 26.6.1942 and Bromley to
    Brittain 9.9.1944 TNA CAB 301/97.
11 Brig Petrie to Col Wood 26.5.1944 TNA KV 4/223.
12 West and Tsarev, 1999, pp. 303-04.
13 Wichhart, 2011, p. 824.
14 Baxter's minute 14.5.1943 TNA FO 371/35020; Col Wood to
    CICI officers, June 1944 TNA FO 624/66.
15 Anni's diary 18.2.1944 Stockholm Collection.
16 Philby, 1968, pp. 114-25; Robert Cecil, "A few home truths about
    Philby's Silent War", *The Times*, London, 2.2.1978; Jeffery, 2010,
    p. 486.
17 For more details of Torma's activities see Tamman, 2011, pp.
    143-45.
18 Galsworthy minute 9.4.1945 TNA FO 371/47044 N3599/958/59.
19 Anni to Ants 28.12.1944 EKM EKLA 237/M53:3.
20 Anni to mother 3.10.1944 EKN EKLA 237/M53:3.

21 Public Safety Branch director to military secretary at
    Commissioner's Office 9.11.1944 Stockholm Collection.
22 Brian to Anni 12.4.1946 Stockholm Collection.

Chapter 10 Denazification of post-war Germany

1   See TNA FO 1005/623 for the minutes of the PS Committee and
    1005/635 for the minutes of the NAD sub-committee.
2   Minutes of meeting 31.8.1945 TNA FO 1005/635.
3   Minutes of the NAD Sub-Committee meeting 9.11.1945 TNA FO
    1005/635.
4   The scanty 9 November minutes do not confirm the progress
    evident from Brian's jubilant tone. See minutes of meetings on
    9.11.1945 and 13.11.1945 TNA FO 1005/635.
5   Brian to Anni 20.4.1946 Stockholm Collection.
6   Smith, 1999, p. 267.
7   Ibid., p. 261.
8   Minutes of meetings 13.9.1945 and 11.10.1945 TNA FO
    1005/635.
9   Brian to Anni 23.4.1946 Stockholm Collection.
10 Brian to Anni 12.4.1946 Stockholm Collection.
11 Brian to Anni 16.4.1946 Stockholm Collection.
12 Undated document signed by Eric G. Webber, deputy assistant
    inspector general, Public Safety Branch, Stockholm Collection.
13 Brian to unidentified friend in 1947 Stockholm Collection.
14 Brian to unidentified friend spring 1948 Stockholm Collection.
15 Ibid.
16 Brian to Ants, May 1948 Stockholm Collection.
17 Brian to Ants 3.1.1949, University of Florida Library, Ants Oras
    correspondence, series 62, box 7.
18 Ants to Prof Robertson 6.1.1949, University of Florida Library,
    Ants Oras correspondence, series 62, box 7.
19 *Aruanne*, 2005, p. 37.
20 Brian to unidentified friend in 1948 Stockholm Collection.
21 Brian to Anni, 1949 Stockholm Collection.
22 Brian in London to Anni in Teignmouth in early 1949 Stockholm
    Collection.

23   Brian to Anni, July 1949 Stockholm Collection.
24   Brian to unidentified friend in Feb 1953 Stockholm Collection.

Chapter 11   Afterthoughts

1   Anni's diary 17.3.1968 Stockholm Collection.
2   Bryn from Bron, in the Swallow's Nest, 14 February 1948
     Stockholm Collection.
3   Brian to Anni Sept 1947 while she was visiting family in
     Sweden, Stockholm Collection.
4   Anni's diary 13.1.1943 Stockholm Collection.
5   Brian to unidentified friend in 1952 Stockholm Collection.
6   Brian to unidentified friend in 1951 Stockholm Collection.
7   Brian to unidentified friend in 1953 Stockholm Collection.
8   Brian's diary 7.6.1917 Stockholm Collection.
9   Brian to Anni in 1949 Stockholm Collection.
10   Brian to Anni 16.9.1952 Stockholm Collection.
11   Anni's diary 20.9.1952 Stockholm Collection.
12   Jeffery, 2010, p. 191; David Mure to Gulzar Ahmed 31.10.1980
     IWM, Mure papers, box 2.
13   Brian to Anni 8.10.1941 Stockholm Collection.
14   "The horrors of Bolshevism", *The Times*, 14.11.1919; "Taras
     Shevchenko", *Ukrainian Review*, London, March 1955.
15   Obituary of Lt-Col C.K.O.B. Giffey, *Firm*, January 1968.

Bibliography

Primary sources

Army Personnel Centre (APC), Glasgow

Estonian Film Archives (EFA), Tallinn

Estonian Historical Archive (EAA), Tartu

Estonian Literary Museum (KLM), Tartu

Estonian State Archives (ERA, ERAF), Tallinn

Giffey papers, Stockholm

Imperial War Museum (IWM), London

National Archives (TNA), London

Oxford University Archives, Oxford

University of Florida Library, Gainesville

US National Archives (NARA), College Park

Books and journal articles

Andrew, Christopher, *Secret Service. The Making of the British Intelligence Community*, London, 1992.

Andrew, Christopher and Gordievsky, Oleg, *KGB: The Inside Story of Its Foreign Operations from Lenin to Gorbachev*, New York, 1991.

Andrew, Christopher and Mitrokhin, Vasili, *The Mitrokhin Archive II: The KGB and the World*, London, 2005.

Aruanne Eesti NSV Ministrite Nõukogu juures asuva Riikliku Julgeoleku Komitee 2.vastuluureosakonna tööst 1955.aastal (Report to the KGB at the Estonian SSR Council of Ministers on the work of 2nd department, counter-intelligence, in 1955), Tallinn, 1998.

Aruanne ENSV Ministrite Nõukogu juures asuva Riikliku Julgeolekukomitee 2.vastuluureosakonna tööst ajavahemikul 1.4.1954-1.4.1955 (Report to the KGB at the Estonian SSR Council of Ministers on the work of 2nd department, counter-intelligence, 1.4.1954-1.4.1955), Tallinn, 1997.

Barton, E.C., *Let the Boy Win His Spurs*, London, 1976.

Batatu, Hanna, *The Old Social Classes and the Revolutionary Movement in Iraq. A Study of Iraq's Old Landed and Commercial Classes and its Communists, Ba'thists and Free Officers*, Princeton, 1978.

Benton, Peggie, *Baltic Countdown*, London, 1984.

Birdwood, Lt-Col Lord, *The Worcestershire Regiment 1922-1950*, Aldershot, 1952.

Blunck, Hans Friedrich, *Licht auf den Zügeln*, Mannheim, 1953.

Clive, Nigel, *A Greek Experience 1943-1948*, Salisbury, 1985.

Dovey, H.O., "Maunsell and Mure", *Intelligence and National Security*, Vol 8, No 1, Jan 1993.

Greene, Graham, *Ways of Escape*, London, 1999.

Greene, Richard (ed.), *Graham Greene: A Life in Letters*, London, 2008.

Gregory, J.D., *On the Edge of Diplomacy. Rambles and Reflections 1902-1928*, London, 1929.

Hinsley, F.H. et al, *British Intelligence in the Second World War: Its Influence on Strategy and Operations. Volume One*, London, 1979.

Hinsley, F.H. and Simkins, C.A.G., *British Intelligence in the Second World War. Volume Four. Security and Counter-Intelligence*, London, 1990.

Ilmjärv, Magnus (comments), *President ja sõjavägede ülemjuhataja NKVD ees, dokumendid ja materjalid* (The President and commander-in-chief before the NKVD: documents and materials), Tallinn, 1999.

Jeffery, Keith, *MI6: The History of the Secret Intelligence Service 1909-1949*, London, 2010.

Jürjo, Indrek, *Pagulus ja Nõukogude Eesti: vaateid KGB, EKP ja VEKSA arhiividokumentide põhjal* (Emigration and Soviet Estonia: observations based on archival documents of the KGB, Estonian Communist Party and the Association for Friendship with Estonians abroad), Tallinn, 1996.

Lucas, Edward, *Deception: Spies, Lies and How Russia Dupes the West*, London, 2012.

Luts, Alfred, *Heitluste keerises* (In the thick of fighting), Tallinn, 2004.

Macintyre, Ben, *A Spy Among Friends: Kim Philby and the Great Betrayal*, London, 2014.

Milne, Tim, *Kim Philby: The Unknown Story of the KGB's Master-Spy*, London, 2014.

Mockler, Anthony, *Graham Greene: Three Lives*, Angus, 1994.

Mothander, Carl, *Parunid, eestlased ja enamlased* (Barons, Estonians and Bolsheviks), Tartu, 1998.

Mure, David, *Master of Deception: Tangled Webs in London and the Middle East*, London, 1980.

Mure, David, *Practise to Deceive*, London, 1977.

My Silent War. The Autobiography of Kim Philby, London, 1968.

Niidassoo, Külli and Ohmann, Valdur, "Eestimaa Kommunistlik Partei – 1930. aastad kuni juuli 1940" (Estonian Communist Party – the 1930s until July 1940), *Tuna*, Tallinn, No 3, 2000.

Paas, Heini, *Ferdi Sannamees*, Tallinn, 1974.

Philby, Kim, *My Silent War*, New York, 1968.

Pullat, Raimo, *Versailles'st Westerplatteni: Eesti ja Poola suhted kahe maailmasõja vahel* (From Versailles to Westerplatte: Estonian-Polish interwar relations), Tallinn, 2001.

Roolaht, A., *Nii see oli... Kroonika ühest unustuseliiva maetud ajastust* (How it was... Chronicle of a forgotten era), Tallinn, 1990.

Smith, Michael, *Foley: The Spy Who Saved 10,000 Jews*, London, 1999.

Stacke, H. FitzMaurice, *The Worcestershire Regiment in the Great War*, Vol I, Kiddeminster, 2002.

Stepan Anastasovich Mikoyan: An Autobiography, Shrewsbury, 1999.

Stirling, Tessa et al (eds.), *Intelligence Co-operation Between Poland and Great Britain During World War II. Vol. I: The Report of the Anglo-Polish Historical Committee*, London and Portland, 2005.

Tamman, Tina, *The Last Ambassador: August Torma, Soldier, Diplomat, Spy*, Amsterdam and New York, 2011.

Tarvel, Enn (ed.), *Luuramisi* (Spying), Tallinn, 1999.

Tolley, Kemp, *Caviar and Commissars*, Annapolis, 1983.

Tomaselli, Phil, *Tracing Your Secret Service Ancestors*, Barnsley, 2009.

Walter, Hannes, "Uprising of December 1, 1924", *Baltic Defence Review*, Tartu, 1999.

Wark, Wesley K., "'Our Man in Riga': Reflections on the SIS Career and Writings of Leslie Nicholson", *Intelligence and National Security*, Vol 11, No 4, Oct 1996.

West, Nigel, *MI6: British Secret Intelligence Service Operations 1909-45*, London, Glasgow, Toronto, Sydney and Auckland, 1987.

West, Nigel, *The A to Z of British Intelligence*, Lanham, Toronto and Plymouth, 2009.

West, Nigel and Tsarev, Oleg, *The Crown Jewels: The British Secrets Exposed by the KGB Archives*, London, 1999.

West, Nigel and Tsarev, Oleg (eds.), *Triplex: Secrets from the Cambridge Spies*, New Haven and London, 2009.

Whitwell, John, *British Agent*, London, 1966.

Wichhart, Stefanie K., "A 'New Deal' for the Kurds: Britain's Kurdish Policy in Iraq, 1941-45", *The Journal of Imperial and Commonwealth History*, Vol 39, No 5, Dec 2011.

Wolff, D. and Moullec, G., *Le KGB et les Pays Baltes: 1939-1991*, Paris, 2005.

Index

About the author

Tina Tamman is a journalist who worked for BBC Monitoring for nearly 20 years, handling Estonian and Russian news material. She obtained a PhD from the University of Glasgow in 2010 and her thesis was published by Rodopi as *The Last Ambassador: August Torma, Soldier, Diplomat, Spy*. She lives in Reading but travels frequently to Estonia where she runs an annual essay competition to encourage independent thinking.